The Short St...

GENERAL EDITOR

ADVENT...

MUFFAT

ANIMAL

DETECTION

HORROR

HUMOUR

LOVE

SCIENCE FICTION

SEA

SPORT

SUPERNATURAL

TRAVEL

WESTERN

Animal

This book is due for return on or before the last date shown below.

John Murray
Albemarle Street London

Printed and bound in Great Britain
by Butler & Tanner Ltd,
Frome and London

0 7195 3663 4

CONTENTS

Liam O'Flaherty

His First Flight

The young seagull was alone on his ledge. His two brothers and his sister had already flown away the day before. He had been afraid to fly with them. Somehow when he had taken a little run forward to the brink of the ledge and attempted to flap his wings he became afraid. The great expanse of sea stretched down beneath, and it was such a long way down—miles down. He felt certain that his wings would never support him, so he bent his head and ran away back to the little hole under the ledge where he slept at night. Even when each of his brothers and his little sister, whose wings were far shorter than his own, ran to the brink, flapped their wings, and flew away he failed to muster up courage to take that plunge which appeared to him so desperate. His father and mother had come around calling to him shrilly, upbraiding him, threatening to let him starve on his ledge unless he flew away. But for the life of him he could not move.

That was twenty-four hours ago. Since then nobody had come near him. The day before, all day long, he had watched his parents flying about with his brothers and sisters, perfecting them in the art of flight, teaching them how to skim the waves and dive for fish. He had, in fact, seen his older brother catch his first herring and devour it, standing on a rock, while his parents circled around raising a proud cackle. And all the morning the whole family had walked about on the big plateau midway down the opposite cliff, taunting him with his cowardice.

The sun was now ascending the sky, blazing warmly on his ledge that faced the south. He felt the heat because he had not eaten since the previous nightfall. Then he had found a dried piece of mackerel's tail at the far end of his ledge. Now there was not a single scrap of food left. He had searched every inch, rooting among the rough, dirt-caked straw nest where he and his brothers and sister had been hatched. He even gnawed at the dried pieces of spotted-eggshell. It was like eating part of himself. He had then trotted back and forth from one end of the ledge to the other, his grey body the colour of the cliff, his long grey legs stepping daintily, trying to find some means of reaching his parents without having to fly. But on each side of him the ledge ended in a sheer fall of precipice, with the sea beneath. And between him and his parents there was a deep wide chasm. Surely he could reach them without flying if he could only move northwards along the cliff face? But then on what could he walk? There was no ledge, and he was not a fly. And above him he could see nothing. The precipice was sheer, and the top of it was perhaps farther away than the sea beneath him.

He stepped slowly out to the brink of the ledge, and, standing on one leg with the other leg hidden under his wing, he closed one eye, then the other, and pretended to be falling asleep. Still they took no notice of him. He saw his two brothers and his sister lying on the plateau dozing, with their heads sunk into their necks. His father was preening the feathers on his white back. Only his mother was looking at him. She was standing on a little high hump on the plateau, her white breast thrust forward. Now and again she tore at a piece of fish that lay at her feet, and then scraped each side of her beak on the rock. The sight of the food maddened him. How he loved to tear that food that way, scraping his beak now and again to whet it! He uttered a low cackle. His mother cackled too, and looked over at him.

'Ga, ga, ga,' he cried, begging her to bring him over some food.

'Gaw-ool-ah,' she screamed back derisively. But he kept calling plaintively, and after a minute or so he uttered a joyful scream. His mother had picked up a piece of fish and was flying across to him with it. He leaned out eagerly, tapping the rock with his feet, trying to get nearer to her as she flew across. But when she was just opposite him, abreast of the ledge, she halted, her legs hanging limp, her wings motionless, the piece of fish in her beak almost within reach of his beak. He waited a moment in surprise, wondering why she did not come nearer, and then, maddened by hunger, he dived at the fish. With a loud scream, he fell outwards and downwards into space. His mother had swooped upwards. As he passed beneath her he heard the swish of her wings. Then a monstrous terror seized him and his heart stood still. He could hear nothing. But it only lasted a moment. The next moment he felt his wings spread outwards. The wind rushed against his breast feathers, then under his stomach and against his wings. He could feel the tip of his wings cutting the air. He was not falling headlong now. He was soaring gradually downwards and outwards. He was no longer afraid. He just felt a bit dizzy. Then he flapped his wings once and he soared upwards. He uttered a joyous scream and flapped them again. He soared higher. He raised his breast and banked against the wind. 'Ga, ga, ga. Ga, ga, ga. Gaw-ool-ah.' His mother swooped past him, her wings making a loud noise. He answered her with another scream. Then his father flew over him screaming. Then he saw his two brothers and his sister flying around him curveting and banking and soaring and diving. Then he completely forgot that he had not always been able to fly, and commenced himself to dive and soar and curvet, shrieking shrilly.

He was near the sea now, flying straight over it, facing straight out over the sea, over the ocean. He saw a vast green sea beneath him, with little ridges moving over it, and he turned his beak sideways and crowed amusedly. His parents and his brothers and sister had landed on this green floor in front of him. They were beckoning to him, calling shrilly. He dropped his legs to stand on the green sea. His legs sank into it. He screamed with fright and attempted to rise again, flapping his wings. But he was tired and weak with hunger and he could not rise, exhausted by the strange exercise. His feet sank into the green sea, and then his belly touched it and he sank no farther. He was floating on it. And around him his family was screaming, praising him, and their beaks were offering him scraps of dog fish.

He had made his first flight.

Charles G. D. Roberts

How a Cat Played Robinson Crusoe

The island was a mere sandbank off the low, flat coast. Not a tree broke its bleak levels—not even a shrub. But the long gritty stalks of the marsh grass clothed it everywhere above tidemark; and a tiny rivulet of sweet water, flowing from a spring at its centre, drew a ribbon of inland herbage and tenderer green across the harsh and sombre yellow grey of the grass. Few would have chosen the island as a place to live, yet at its seaward end, where the changing tides were never still, stood a spacious, one-storey, wide-verandaed cottage, with a low shed behind it. The virtue of this lone plot of sand was coolness. When the neighbouring mainland would be sweltering day and night alike under a breathless heat, out here on the island there was always a cool wind blowing. Therefore a wise city dweller had appropriated the sea waif and built his summer home thereon, where the tonic airs might bring back the rose to the pale cheeks of his children.

The family came to the island towards the end of June. In the first week of September they went away, leaving every door and window of house and shed securely shuttered, bolted or barred against the winter's storms. A roomy boat, rowed by two fishermen, carried them across the half mile of racing tides that separated them from the mainland. The elders of the household were not sorry to get back to the world of men, after two months of mere wind, and sun, and waves, and waving grass tops. But the children went with tear-stained faces. They were leaving behind them their favourite pet, the accustomed comrade of their migrations, a handsome, moon-faced cat, striped like a tiger. The animal had mysteriously disappeared two days before, vanishing from the face of the island without leaving a trace behind. The only reasonable explanation seemed to be that she had been snapped up by a passing eagle. The cat, meanwhile, was fast prisoner at the other end of the island, hidden beneath a broken barrel and some hundredweight of drifted sand.

The old barrel, with the staves battered out of one side, had stood, half buried, on the crest of a sand ridge raised by a long prevailing wind. Under its lee the cat had found a sheltered hollow, full of sun, where she had been wont to lie curled up for hours at a time, basking and sleeping. Meanwhile the sand had been steadily piling itself higher and higher behind the unstable barrier. At last it had piled too high; and suddenly, before a stronger gust, the barrel had come toppling over beneath a mass of sand, burying the sleeping cat out of sight and light. But at the same time the sound half of the barrel had formed a safe roof to her prison, and she was neither crushed nor smothered. When the children in their anxious search all over the island chanced upon the mound of fine, white sand they gave it but one careless look. They could not hear the faint cries that came, at intervals, from the close darkness within. So they went away sorrowfully, little dreaming that their friend was imprisoned almost beneath their feet.

For three days the prisoner kept up her appeals for help. On the third day the wind changed and presently blew up a gale. In a few hours it had uncovered the barrel. At one corner a tiny spot of light appeared.

Eagerly the cat stuck her paw through the hole. When she withdrew it again the hole was much enlarged. She took the hint and fell to scratching. At first her efforts were rather aimless; but presently, whether by good luck or quick sagacity, she learned to make her scratching more effective. The opening rapidly enlarged, and at last she was able to squeeze her way out.

The wind was tearing madly across the island, filled with flying sand. The seas hurled themselves trampling up the beach, with the uproar of a bombardment. The grasses lay bowed flat in long quivering ranks. Over the turmoil the sun stared down from a deep, unclouded blue. The cat, when first she met the full force of the gale, was fairly blown off her feet. As soon as she could recover herself she crouched low and darted into the grasses for shelter. But there was little shelter there, the long stalks being held down almost level. Through their lashed lines, however, she sped straight before the gale, making for the cottage at the other end of the island, where she would find, as she fondly imagined, not only food and shelter but also loving comfort to make her forget her terrors.

Still and desolate in the bright sunshine and the tearing wind the house frightened her. She could not understand the tight-closed shutters, the blind, unresponsive doors that would no longer open to her anxious appeal. The wind swept her savagely across the naked veranda. Climbing with difficulty to the dining-room windowsill, where so often she had been let in, she clung there a few moments and yowled heartbrokenly. Then, in a sudden panic, she jumped down and ran to the shed. That, too, was closed, and she could not understand it. Cautiously she crept around the foundations—but those had been built honestly: there was no such thing as getting in that way. On every side it was nothing but a blank, forbidding face that the old familiar house confronted her with.

The cat had always been so coddled and pampered by the children that she had had no need to forage for herself; but, fortunately for her, she had learned to hunt the marsh mice and grass sparrows for amusement. So now, being ravenous from her long fast under the sand, she slunk mournfully away from the deserted house and crept along the lee of a sand ridge to a little grassy hollow which she knew. Here the gale caught only the tops of the grasses; and here, in the warmth and comparative calm, the furry little marsh folk, mice and shrews, were going about their business undisturbed.

The cat, quick and stealthy, soon caught one and eased her hunger. She caught several. And then, making her way back to the house, she spent hours in heartsick prowling around and around it, sniffing and peering, yowling piteously on the threshold and windowsill; and every now and then being blown ignominiously across the smooth, naked expanse of the veranda floor. At last, hopelessly discouraged, she curled herself up beneath the children's window and went to sleep.

In spite of her loneliness and grief the life of the island prisoner during the next two or three weeks was by no means one of hardship. Besides her abundant food of birds and mice she quickly learned to catch tiny fish in the mouth of the rivulet, where salt water and fresh water met. It was an exciting game, and she became expert at dashing the grey tom-cod and blue-and-silver sand-lance far up the slope with a sweep of her armed paw. But when the equinoctial storms roared down upon the island, with furious rain, and low, black clouds torn to shreds, then life became more difficult for her. Game all took to cover, where it was hard to find. It was difficult to get around in the drenched and lashing grass; and, moreover, she loathed wet. Most of the time she went hungry, sitting sullen and desolate under the lee of the house, glaring out defiantly at the rush and battling tumult of the waves.

The storm lasted nearly ten days before it blew itself clean out. On the eighth day the abandoned wreck of a small Nova Scotia schooner drove ashore, battered out of all likeness to a ship. But hulk as it was it had passengers of a sort. A horde of rats got through the surf and scurried into the hiding of the grass roots. They promptly made themselves at home, burrowing under the grass and beneath old, half-buried timbers, and carrying panic into the ranks of the mice and shrews.

When the storm was over the cat had a decided surprise in her first long hunting expedition. Something had rustled the grass heavily and she trailed it, expecting a particularly large, fat marsh mouse. When she pounced and alighted upon an immense old ship's rat, many-voyaged and many-battled, she got badly bitten. Such an experience had never before fallen to her lot. At first she felt so injured that she was on the point of backing out and running away. Then her latent pugnacity awoke, and the fire of far-off ancestors. She flung herself into the fight with a rage that took no accounting of the wounds she got; and the struggle was soon over. Her wounds, faithfully licked, quickly healed themselves in that clean and tonic air; and after that, having learned how to handle such big game, she no more got bitten.

During the first full moon after her abandonment—the first week in October—the island was visited by still weather with sharp night frosts. The cat discovered then that it was most exciting to hunt by night and do her sleeping in the daytime. She found that now, under the strange whiteness of the moon, all her game was astir— except the birds, which had fled to the mainland during the storm, gathering for the southward flight. The blanched grasses, she found, were now everywhere a-rustle; and everywhere dim little shapes went darting with thin squeaks across ghostly-white sands. Also she made the acquaintance of a new bird, which she regarded at first uneasily and then with vengeful wrath. This was the brown marsh owl, which came over from the mainland to do some autumn mouse hunting. There were two pairs of these big, downy-winged, round-eyed hunters, and they did not know there was a cat on the island.

The cat, spying one of them as it swooped soundlessly hither and thither over the silvered grass tops, crouched with flattened ears. With its wide spread of wing it looked bigger than herself; and the great round face, with hooked beak and wild, staring eyes, appeared extremely formidable. However, she was no coward; and presently, though not without reasonable caution, she went about her hunting. Suddenly the owl caught a partial glimpse of her in the grass—probably of her ears or head. He swooped; and at the same instant she sprang upward to meet the assault, spitting and growling harshly and striking with unsheathed claws. With a frantic flapping of his great wings the owl checked himself and drew back into the air, just escaping the clutch of those indignant claws. After that the marsh owls were careful to give her a wide berth. They realized that the black-striped animal with the quick spring and the clutching claws was not to be interfered with. They perceived that she was some relation to that ferocious prowler, the lynx.

In spite of all this hunting, however, the furry life of the marsh grass was so teeming, so inexhaustible, that the depredations of cat, rats and owls were powerless to make more than a passing impression upon it. So the hunting and the merrymaking went on side by side under the indifferent moon.

As the winter deepened–with bursts of sharp cold and changing winds that forced the cat to be continually changing her refuge— she grew more and more unhappy. She felt her homelessness keenly. Nowhere on the whole island could she find a nook where she might feel secure from both wind and rain. As for the old barrel, the first cause of her misfortunes, there was no help in that. The winds had long ago turned it completely over, open to the sky, then drifted it full of sand and reburied it. And in any case the cat would have been afraid to go near it again. So it came about that she alone of all the island dwellers had no shelter to turn to when the real winter arrived, with snows that smothered the grass tops out of sight, and frosts that lined the shore with grinding ice cakes. The rats had their holes under the buried fragments of wreckage; the mice and shrews had their deep, warm tunnels; the owls had nests in hollow trees far away in the forests of the mainland. But the cat, shivering and frightened, could do nothing but crouch against the blind walls of the unrelenting house and let the snow whirl itself and pile itself about her.

And now, in her misery, she found her food cut off. The mice ran secure in their hidden runways, where the grass roots on each side of them gave them easy and abundant provender. The rats, too, were out of sight—digging burrows themselves in the soft snow in the hope of intercepting some of the tunnels of the mice, and now and then snapping up an unwary passerby. The ice fringe, crumbling and heaving under the ruthless tide, put an end to her fishing. She would have tried to capture one of the formidable owls in her hunger, but the owls no longer came to the island. They would return, no doubt, later in the season when the snow had hardened and the mice had begun to come out and play on the surface. But for the present they were following an easier chase in the deeps of the upland forest.

When the snow stopped falling and the sun came out again there fell such keen cold as the cat had never felt before. The day, as it chanced, was Christmas; and if the cat had had any idea as to the calendar she would certainly have marked the day in her memory as it was an eventful one for her. Starving as she was she could not sleep, but kept ceaselessly on the prowl. This was fortunate, for had she gone to sleep without any more shelter than the wall of the house she would never have wakened again. In her restlessness she wandered to the farther side of the island where, in a somewhat sheltered and sunny recess of the shore facing the mainland, she found a patch of bare sand, free of ice cakes and just uncovered by the tide. Opening upon this recess were the tiny entrances to several of the mouse tunnels.

Close beside one of these holes in the snow the cat crouched, quiveringly intent. For ten minutes or more she waited, never so much as twitching a whisker. At last a mouse thrust out its little pointed head. Not daring to give it time to change its mind or take alarm she pounced. The mouse, glimpsing the doom ere it fell, doubled back upon itself in the narrow runway. Hardly realizing what she did in her desperation the cat plunged head and shoulders into the snow, reaching blindly after the vanished prize. By great good luck she caught it.

It was her first meal in four bitter days. The children had always tried to share with her their Christmas cheer and enthusiasm, and had usually succeeded in interesting her by an agreeable lavishness in the matter of cream; but never before had she found a Christmas feast so good.

Now she had learned a lesson. Being naturally clever and her wits sharpened by her fierce necessities, she had grasped the idea that it was possible to follow her prey a little way into the snow. She had not realized that the snow was so penetrable. She had quite wiped out the door of this particular runway; so she went and crouched beside a similar one, but here she had to wait a long time before an adventurous mouse came to peer out. But this time she showed that she had grasped her lesson. It was straight at the side of the entrance that she pounced, where instinct told her that the body of the mouse would be. One outstretched paw thus cut off the quarry's retreat. Her tactics were completely successful; and as her head went plunging into the fluffy whiteness she felt the prize between her paws.

Her hunger now fairly appeased, she found herself immensely excited over this new fashion of hunting. Often before had she waited at mouse holes, but never had she found it possible to break down the walls and invade the holes themselves. It was a thrilling idea. As she crept towards another hole a mouse scurried swiftly up the sand and darted into it. The cat, too late to catch him before he disappeared, tried to follow him. Scratching clumsily but hopefully she succeeded in forcing the full length of her body into the snow. She found no sign of the fugitive, which was by this time racing in safety down some dim transverse tunnel. Her eyes, mouth, whiskers and fur full of the powdery white particles, she backed out, much disappointed. But in that moment she had realized that it was much warmer in there beneath the snow than out in the stinging air. It was a second and vitally important lesson; and though she was probably unconscious of having learned it she instinctively put the new lore into practice a little while later.

Having succeeded in catching yet another mouse for which her appetite made no immediate demand, she carried it back to the house and laid it down in tribute on the veranda steps while she meowed and stared hopefully at the desolate, snow-draped door. Getting no response she carried the mouse down with her to the hollow behind the drift which had been caused by the bulging front of the bay-window on the end of the house. Here she curled herself up forlornly, thinking to have a wink of sleep.

But the still cold was too searching. She looked at the sloping wall of snow beside her and cautiously thrust her paw into it. It was very soft and light. It seemed to offer practically no resistance. She pawed away in an awkward fashion till she had scooped out a sort of tiny cave. Gently she pushed herself into it, pressing back the snow on every side till she had room to turn around.

Then turn around she did several times, as dogs do in getting their beds arranged to their liking. In this process she not only packed down the snow beneath her, but she also rounded out for herself a snug chamber with a comparatively narrow doorway. From this snowy retreat she gazed forth with a solemn air of possession; then she went to sleep with a sense of comfort, of 'homeyness,' such as she had never before felt since the disappearance of her friends.

Having thus conquered misfortune and won herself the freedom of the winter wild, her life though strenuous was no longer one of any terrible hardship. With patience at the mouse holes she could catch enough to eat; and in her snowy den she slept warm and secure. In a little while, when a crust had formed over the surface, the mice took to coming out at night and holding revels on the snow. Then the owls, too, came back; and the cat, having tried to catch one, got sharply bitten and clawed before she realized the propriety of letting it go. After this experience she decided that owls, on the whole, were meant to be let alone. But for all that she found it fine hunting, out there on the bleak, unfenced, white reaches of the snow.

Thus, mistress of the situation, she found the winter slipping by without further serious trials. Only once, towards the end of January, did Fate send her another bad quarter of an hour. On the heels of a peculiarly bitter cold snap a huge white owl from the Arctic Barrens came one night to the island. The cat, taking observations from the corner of the veranda, caught sight of him. One look was enough to assure her that this was a very different kind of visitor from the brown marsh owls. She slipped inconspicuously down into her burrow; and until the great white owl went away, some twenty-four hours later, she kept herself discreetly out of sight.

When spring came back to the island, with the nightly shrill chorus of fluting frogs in the shallow, sedgy pools and the young grass alive with nesting birds, the prisoner's life became almost luxurious in its easy abundance. But now she was once more homeless, since her snug den had vanished with the snow. This did not much matter to her, however, for the weather grew warmer and more tranquil day by day; and moreover, she herself, in being forced back upon her instincts, had learned to be as contented as a tramp. Nevertheless, with all her capacity for learning and adapting herself she had not forgotten anything. So when, one day in June, a crowded boat came over from the mainland, and children's voices, clamouring across the grass tops, broke the desolate silence of the island, the cat heard and sprang up out of her sleep on the veranda steps.

For one second she stood, listening intently. Then, almost as a dog would have done, and as few of her supercilious tribe ever condescend to do, she went racing across to the landing place—to be snatched up into the arms of four happy children at once, and to have her fine fur ruffled to a state which it would cost her an hour's assiduous toilet to put in order.

Way-atcha the Coon-Raccoon of Kilder Creek

March, with its ranks of crows and rolling drum calls from the woodwale, was coming in different moods to own the woods. The sun had gone, and a soft starlight on the slushy snow was bright enough for the keen eyes of the wood-prowlers. Two of them came; quickly they passed along a lying trunk, through the top of the fallen tree, across the snow to follow each convenient log as a sort of sidewalk. They were large animals—that is, larger than a Fox—of thick form with bushy tails on which the keen night eyes of a passing Owl could see the dark bars, the tribal flag of their kind.

The leader was smaller than the other, and at times showed a querulous impatience, a disposition to nip at the big one following, and yet seemed not to seek escape. The big one came behind with patient forbearance. The singing woodsman, had he seen them, would have understood: these were mates. Obedient to the animal rule, all arrangements for the coming brood were in the mother's control. She must go forth to seek the nursing den; she must know the very time; she alone is pilot of this cruise. He is there merely to fight in case they meet some foe.

Down through the alder thicket by the stream and underbush, and on till they reached the great stretch of timber that was left because the land was low and poor. Much of it was ancient growth, and the Coon-Raccoon—the mother soon to be—passed quickly from one great trunk to another, seeking, seeking—what?

The woodsman knows that a hollow pine is rare, a hollow maple often happens, and a hollow basswood is the rule. He might have found the harbouring trunk in broad daylight, for a hollow tree has a dead top, but in the gloom the Coon seemed to go from one great column to the next with certainty, and knew without climbing them if they were not for her; and at last by the bend where the creek and river join, she climbed the huge dead maple, like one who knows.

This is the perfect lodgment of Coon-Raccoon—high up some mighty, towering tree in some deep, dangerous swamp, near running water with its magic and its foods, a large, convenient chamber, dry and lined with softest rotten wood, a tight-fit door-way, and near it some great branch which gets the sun's full blaze in day. This is the perfect home, and this was what the mother Coon had found.

In April the brood had come, five little ones, ring-tailed and black-masked like their parents. Their baby time was gone, and now in June they were old enough to come out on bright days, and sit in a row on the big limb that was their sunning place. Very early in life their individual characters appeared. There was the timid one whose tail was a ring too short, the fat grey one that was last to leave the nest, and the black-masked one who was big, restless, and ready to do anything but keep quiet, the one that afterwards was named Way-atcha. In their cuddling nursery days the rules of Coon life are simple. Eat, grow, keep quiet—all the rest is mother's business. But once they are old enough to leave the nest they begin to have experiences and learn the other rules.

The sunning perch was free for all, and the youngsters were allowed to climb higher in the tree among the small branches, but below the nest was a great expanse of trunk without any bark on, and quite smooth, a very difficult and dangerous place to climb, and whenever one of the youngsters made a move downward, mother ordered him back in sharp, angry tones.

Way-atcha (his mother called him 'Wirrr' the same as the others, but with a little more vigour to it) had been warned back twice or thrice, but that made him more eager to try the forbidden climb. His mother was inside as he slid below the sunning limb on the rough bark, and on to the smooth trunk. It was twenty times too big for his arms to grip, and down he went, clutching at anything within reach—crash, scramble, down, down, down, and splash into the deep water below.

Startled by the sudden gasp of the others, the mother hurried forth to see her eldest splashing in the brook. She hurried to the rescue, but the stream lodged him against a sandbar, he scrambled out little the worse, and made for the home tree. Mother was half-way down, but seeing him climb she returned to the row of eager faces on the branch above.

Way-atcha went up bravely till he reached the tall smooth trunk where there was no bark, and here he absolutely failed, and giving way to his despair, uttered a long, whining whimper. Mother was back at the hole, but she turned now and coming down, took Way-atcha by the neck rather roughly, placed him between her own forelegs, carried him round the smooth trunk to the side where there were two cracks that gave a claw-hold, and there boosted and kept him from falling while she spanked him all the way home.

It was two weeks later or more before mother judged it time to take them down into the big world, and then she waited for a full moon. Old Coons can do very well on a black night, but they need some light, especially at the beginning of the young one's training.

Father went down first to be ready, in case some enemy was near, and now the youngsters were taught the trick of the smooth trunk. There was only one place to climb it safely: that was where the two cracks made it possible to get clawholds well apart. Mother went first to show the way, and the youngsters followed behind.

Everything was new and surprising to them, everything had to be smelt and handled, stones, logs, grass, the ground, the mud, and, above all things, the water. The bright uncatchable water was puzzling to all except of course Way-atcha who knew, or thought he knew it, already.

The youngsters were full of glee, they chased each other along logs and tumbled each other into little holes, but mother had brought them for something more serious. They had to get their first lesson in earning a living, and this she gave them mainly by example.

Have you ever seen a Coon feeding? His way is to stand by a pool, put in both hands, groping in the mud with quick and sensitive fingers, hunting for frogs, fish, crabs, etc., while his eyes rove the woods far and near, right and left, to look for other chances or to guard against possible enemies. This was mother's way, and the youngsters looked on, more interested in the catch than in the mode.

Then they crowded up close to see better, which meant they lined up along the water's edge. It was so natural to put their hands in the water that at once they were doing as mother did. What a curious sensation to feel the mud sliding between one's fingers; then perhaps a root like a string, then a round soft root that *wriggles*. What a thrill it gives! For instinctively one knows that *that is game*, that is what we are here for. And Way-atcha, who made the find, clutched the pollywog without being told, seized it in his teeth and got *chiefly* a mouthful of mud and sand. He sputtered out everything, mud, pollywog, and all. Mother took the flopping silverbelly, gravely washed it in the clear water, and gave it back to

be gobbled by Way-atcha. Now he knew. Thenceforth he dropped
easily into the habit of his race, and every bite was religiously
washed and cleaned before being eaten. The shy brother with the
short tail was too timid to go far from mother, and what he learned
was little. The other two were quarrelling over a perfectly worthless
old bone. Each 'found it first', and the winner had a barren victory.
Greyback was far out on a log over the water, trying to claw out
the reflection of the moon, but Way-atcha, intoxicated by success,
was now keen to keep on hunting. Down along the muddy margin
he paddled, eagerly glancing this way and that, just like mother,
feeling in all the mud, straining it through his fingers, just like
mother, lifting up a double handful to smell, just like mother,
clutching at some worthless root that seemed to wriggle, then
sputtering it out with a growl, just like father. It was fun, every
bit of it, and when at length his active little fingers clutched the
unmistakable smooth and wriggly body of a frog that was hiding
in the mud, Way-atcha got such a thrill of joy that all the hair
on his back stood up, and he gave the warwhoop of the Coon-Raccoon, which is nothing more than a growl and a snort all mixed
up together. It was a moment of triumph, but Way-atcha did not
forget the first lesson, and that frog was washed as clean as water
could make him before the hunter had his feast.

This was intensely exciting, there was limitless joy in view, but
a sudden noise from father changed it all. He had been scouting
far down the river bank while the youngsters played along the creek
near mother. Now he gave a signal that mother knew too well,
a low puff, like 'Foof', followed by a deep grunt. Mother called
the youngsters with a low grunting. They knew nothing at all of
what it was about, but the sense of alarm had spread instantly
among them, and a minute or two later there was a regular proces-
sion of furry balls climbing the great maple, following the two
cracks, right up to tumble into their comfortable bed.

Faraway down the river came a deep booming sound, the roaring of some terrible animal, no doubt. Mother listened to it from
the door. Presently father came scrambling up the trunk a little
wet, because he had swum the river, after laying a trail to take
the enemy away, and had come home by a new road along the
top of a fence, so that no trail was left and the baying of that awful
hound was lost faraway in the woods.

That night Way-atcha had met and felt some of the big things
that shape a Coon's life: the moonlight hunt, the vigilant mother,
the fighting father, the terrible hound, the safe return home pro-

tected by a break in the trail. But he did not think about it. He remembered only the joy of clutching that fat, wriggling, juicy frog, and next night he was eager to be away on another hunt.

Many animals have a sixth sense, a something that warns them that there is danger about, a something that men once had, and called 'a far sense of happenings' or a 'sense of luck'. This seems to be strongest in mothers when they have their young. And when the next night came Way-atcha's mother felt uneasy. There was something wrong. She delayed going down the round stairway and lay watching and listening on the sunning branch till everyone was very cross and hungry. Way-atcha was simply overcome with impatience. Father went down the trunk but soon came up again. The children whimpered, but mother refused to budge. Her quick ears were turned once or twice towards the river, but nothing of note was heard or seen. The moon had set, and at length in the darkest hours the mother led her family down the big trunk. All were hungry, and they rushed heedlessly along the bank, dabbling and splashing. Then Way-atcha caught a frog, and little Ring Short a pollywog. Then all had caught frogs, and it seemed the whole world was one big joyous hunt without a care or a worry.

Now out on a sandbar Way-atcha found a new kind of frog. It looked like two flat bones lying side by side, but the smell was pleasant. He reached out, and at once the two bones closed together on his toes, squeezing them so hard that he squalled out, 'Mother, Mother!' Mother came running to help, of course, while Way-atcha danced up and down in pain and fear. But the old one had seen mussel clams before. She seized the hard thing in her teeth, crushed the hinge side, and ended the trouble. Now Way-atcha had the pleasure of picking out the meat from the sharp bits of shell, washing them clean in the river, and gobbling them as a new kind of frog and everything seemed very well to him.

But father climbed a root and snuffed, sniffed, and listened, and mother studied all the smells and trails that were along the pathway farther from the river bank. She had had little time for hunting. Her secret sense was strong on her, and she gave the signal to return.

The youngsters followed very unwillingly. Way-atcha was almost rebellious. There seemed in his judgement to be every reason for staying and none whatever for going home. But the best of judgement must yield to superior force. Mother's paws were strong and father could be very rough. So the seven fur balls mounted the smooth maple stairway as before.

The Red Fox of the hillside yapped three times, a little song sparrow sang aloud in his dreams not far from the great maple, and the Coon mother heard without heeding. Then later came another sound, quite low and distant, feeble indeed. The young seemed not to hear it, but it set the mother's hair on end. It was a different note, coming from anywhere in the north: the harmless wind made just such noises at times, but in this were also sharp cracks, like blows struck on wood, and once or twice yelps that must have been from dogs.

The sounds came nearer and louder, red stars appeared among the trees, and soon a band of men out with dogs came menacing every living prowler in the woods. The fresh Fox track down below diverted the attention of the dogs so they did not come near the Coon tree, and mother knew that they had escaped a great danger that night.

The following evening Mother Coon looked forty ways and sniffed every breeze that blew, while the moon swung past four trees quite near the door before she would let the family go on their regular hunt. They supposed, of course, she would lead down the usual way by the creek, but she did not. She moved in a new direction upstream, nor would she stop to hunt, but pushed on. They reached a stretch of bank where frogs went jump, jump, at every bank of sedge. It seemed most promising, but mother still pushed on. Then a loud noise like rising wind was heard, only sometimes it splashed like a frog or even a muskrat. Then they came to the thing that made it, the creek itself, jumping over a rocky ledge into a pool, sparkling in the moonrays, noisy in the night. Mother held them back a little while she looked hard ahead and around. Then she crouched; her hair rose up; she growled. Father came alongside. The youngsters had no desire now to rush ahead. There around the water so full of game were other hunters, splashing, catching frogs, and feasting. They were in size like Way-atcha's people, and when the tail of one was turned there surely were the seven rings that make the tribal flag of Coon-Raccoon.

But someone was trespassing. Which family owned this hunting? That is always a serious question in the woods. Father Coon stood up very high on his legs, puffed out his hair, and walked forward from the cover, along the open margin. There was a noisy rush of the other family, then three young in it went whimpering to their mother, and their father stood up high, puffed out his hair, and came marching stiffly and openly towards Way-atcha's father. Each gave a low growl, which meant, 'Here you, get out of this or I'll make you!' Then, since neither got out, they squared up face to face. Each felt that he must protect his family and drive the trespassers away; and so they stood and glared at each other, while the young ones of each crowded closely behind their mothers.

This is the animal law of range. The first finder owns it, if he marks it at leading points, using for this the scent glands near the tail that nature gave for just such purposes. If two hunters have equal claims, they fight, and the stronger holds it. Way-atcha's people, as it chanced, had not marked the hunting ground for weeks, so their musk marks were nearly washed away. The other family came later, but had used it much, and marked it, too. The rival claims were balanced. Nothing now but a fight could settle it.

And this is the Coon's chief mode of fight: close on the enemy, offering the well-defended neck or shoulders to his attack, seize him around the waist and throw him so he will *fall on you*; for the under Coon has the best chance to rip open his enemy's belly with hind claws, which are free; holding him with fore claws which are free, his teeth have free play at the enemy's throat, which is exposed.

So Way-atcha's black-masked sire came edging on, a little side-wise, and the Coon of the Pool having sized up the other as bigger than himself, held back a little, fearing to close at once.

Old Black Mask made a pass; the Pool Coon parried. They dodged round and round, neither gaining nor giving ground. Another pass, then Black Mask's footing slipped, the Pool Coon closed, and the fight was on. But neither got the grip he sought. Their powers were nearly even. They rolled and tugged, while their families squalled, and in a moment both went reeling, and splash, into the deep, cool pool. There is nothing like cool water for cooling. The fighters broke apart, and when they scrambled out they both felt a wonderful change. They had no more desire to fight. Each now was indifferent to the fact that the other was hunting on his grounds. They were in truth cooled off.

There were some angry looks perhaps, and a few low growls, but each with his family set about hunting round the pond, one keeping the thickwood side, the other the open side.

This was the beginning, and in time they all became good friends, for the hunting was plenty for both. The children feasted till their bodies were quite round in front and they were glad once more to climb their big smooth tree.

Way-atcha strongly disapproved of many things his mother did. If she wished to go downstream when his plan was to go up, she must be wrong. If she was hindered by some trifling noise from going to get supper at supper time, it meant senseless annoyance for all. If she was afraid of that curious musky smell on a stone by the shore, well! he was not, and that was all about it.

They had gone for their usual supper hunt one night. After smelling the wind, mother had decided on going down-stream, but Way-atcha had been enjoying visions of the pool with its varied game.

He held back, and when his mother called, he had followed only a little way. Then his keen eyes sighted a movement in the edge of the near water. He sprang on it with the vigour of a growing hunter, and dragged out a fine big crawfish. Then he proceeded to wash it thoroughly and ate it body and bones, not heeding the call of his mother as she led the others away. He was perfectly delighted with himself for this small victory, and felt so set up and independent that he turned in spite of mother's invitation and set out to visit the upper pool as he had planned.

After one or two little captures he reached the jumping water. That very day another visitor had been there. Indian Pete, a trapper, had found the pool, and all about it had seen the tracks of Coon and Muskrat. At this season fur is worthless, but Pete used these creatures for his food, so hid a big steel trap in the mud, and on a little stick farther out in the water he rubbed a rag with a mixture of animal oils and musk.

Ho, ho! there it was again, that very smell that poor timid mother was in such fear of. Now he would examine it. He came down to the place, then sniffed about, yielded to his habit of feeling in the mud as he glanced this way and that, when *snap*, *splash*, and Way-atcha was a prisoner held firmly by one paw in a horrible trap of steel.

Now he thought of his mother, and raised the long soft *whicker* that is the call of his kind, but mother was far away. He himself had made sure of that, and he remembered the clam shell, but all his efforts to pull away or bite off that horrid hard thing were useless; there it clung to his paw, and hanging to it was a sort of strong twisted root that held him there. All night long in vain he whickered, whimpered, and struggled. He was worn out and hoarse as the sun came up, and when Indian Pete came around he was surprised to find in his Muskrat trap a baby Coon, nearly dead with cold and fright, and so weak that he couldn't even bite.

The trapper took the little creature from the trap and put him alive in his pocket, not knowing exactly what he meant to do with him.

On the road home he passed by the Pigott homestead and showed his captive to the children.

The little Coon was still cold and miserable, and when put into the warm arms of the oldest girl he snuggled up so contentedly that he won her heart and she coaxed her father into buying Way-atcha, as the Indian named the captive in his own tongue.

Thus the wanderer found a new and very different home. He was so well taken care of here that in a few days he was all right again. He had children to play with instead of brothers and sisters, and many curious things to eat instead of frogs, but still he loved to dabble his own brown paws in the mud or anything wet whenever he could get the chance. He did not eat milk and bread like a cat or other well-behaved creature; he always put in his paws to fish out the bread, bit by bit, and commonly ended by spilling the milk.

There was one member of the household that Way-atcha held in great fear; that was Roy the sheep-dog, house-dog, watch-dog, and barnyard guard in general. When first they met Roy growled and Way-atcha chirred. Both showed in the bristling shoulder hair that they were deeply moved; each in the smell of the other was instinctively aware of an enemy in an age-long war. The Pigott children had to exercise their right of eminent domain to keep the peace; but the peace was kept. Roy learned to tolerate the Coon in time, the Coon became devotedly fond of Roy, and not two weeks had gone before Way-atcha's usual napping couch was right on Roy's furry breast, deep in the wool, cuddled up with all the dog's four legs drawn close against him.

As he grew stronger he became very mischievous. He seemed half monkey, half kitten, full of fun always, delighted to be petted, and always hungry, and soon learned where to look for dainties. The children used to keep goodies in their pockets for him, and he learned that fact so well that when a stranger came to the house Way-atcha would gravely climb up his legs and seek in all his pockets for something to eat.

On one occasion he had been missing for some hours, always

a suspicious fact. When Mrs Pigott went into the storeroom, stocked now with the summer preserves, she was greeted with the whining call of Way-atcha, more busy than words can tell. There he was wallowing up to his eyes in plum jam, digging down into a crock of it like a washwoman into her tubs, feeling and groping for what? He had gorged himself till he could eat no more, and now prompted by his ancient woodland memories he was groping with his paws among the jam and juice to capture all the plum stones, each in turn to be examined and cast aside. The floor was dotted with stones, the shelf was plastered with the jam of the many pots examined. The Coon was unrecognizable except for his bright eyes and face, but he came waddling, whining, slushing down from the shelf across the floor to climb up Mrs Pigott's dress, assured, he believed, of a cordial welcome. Alas! what a cruel disappointment he got!

One day Mr Pigott set a hen with thirteen eggs. The next day Way-atcha was missing. As they went about calling him by name they heard a faint reply from the hen-house, the gentle 'whicker' that he usually gave in answer. On opening the door, there they saw Way-atcha sprawling on his back in the hen's nest perfectly gorged, and the remains of the thirteen eggs told that he was responsible for a piece of shocking destruction. Roy was the proper guardian of the hen-house. No tramp, no Fox, no Coon from the woods could enter that while he was on guard. But alas! for the conflict of love and duty: in his perplexity the dog had unwittingly followed the plan of a certain great man who said, 'In case of doubt, be friendly.'

Farmer Pigott bore with Way-atcha for long because the children were so fond of the little rascal. But the climax was reached one day when the Coon, left alone in the house, discovered the ink bottle. First he drew the cork and spilled the ink about, then he dabbled his paws in it after his usual manner, and found a new pleasure in laying the inky paws on anything that would take a good paw-mark. At first he made these marks on the table, then he found that the children's school books were just the things and gave much better results. He paw-marked them inside and out, and the incidental joy of dabbling in the wet resulted in frequent re-inking of his paws. Then the wallpaper seemed to need touching up. This led to the window curtains and the girls' dresses, and then as the bedroom door was open Way-atcha scrambled on the bed. It was just beautiful the way that snow-white coverlet took the dear little paw-marks as he galloped over it in great glee. He was several hours alone, and he used up all the ink, so that when the children came in from school it looked as though a hundred little Coons had been running all over the place and leaving black paw-marks. Poor Mrs Pigott actually cried when she saw her beautiful bed, the pride of her heart. But she had to relent when Coonie came running to her just the same as usual, holding out his inky arms and whining '*errr err*' to be taken up and petted as though he were the best little Coon in the world.

But this was too much. Even the children had no excuse to offer; their dresses were ruined. Way-atcha must go; and so it came about that Indian Pete was sent for. Way-atcha did not like the looks of this man, but he had no choice. He was bundled into a sack and taken away by the half-breed, much to Roy's bewilderment, for he disliked the half-breed and despised his dog. Why they should let *that stranger* carry off a member of *his family* was a puzzle. Roy growled a little, sniffed hard at the hunter's legs, and watched him without a tailwag as he went off with the bulging bag.

It was the end of summer now, the Hunting Moon was at hand; the hunter had a new hound to train, and here was the chance to train him on Coon. Way-atcha had no claim on Pete's affection, and nothing educates a dog for Coon so much as taking part in a Coon run and kill.

This was then to be the end of Way-atcha. The trapper would use him, sacrifice him, to train his hunting dog. As he neared his shanty that dog came bounding forth, a lumbering half-breed hound, with a noisy yap which he uttered threefold when he sniffed the sack that held Way-atcha.

And this was the way of the two: in the log stable the Coon was given a box, or little kennel, where he could at least save his life from the dog. Howler was brought in on a chain and encouraged to attack the Coon with loud 'sic hims'. Brave as a lion, seeing so small a foe, he rushed forward, but was held back with the chain, for it was not time for a 'kill'. Many times he charged, to be restrained by his master.

Way-atcha was utterly puzzled. Why should those other two-legged things be so kind and this so hostile? Why should Roy be so friendly and this yellow brute so wicked and cruel? Each time the big dog charged, poor little Way-atcha felt in him the fighting spirit of his valiant race stirred up, and faced the brute snarling and showing all his teeth.

But he would quickly have been done to death by the foe had

not the half-breed held the chain. Only once was the dog allowed to close. He seized the Coon cub by the neck to give the death shake, but nature gave the Coon a strong, loose skin. The shake was scarcely felt, and Way-atcha clamped his teeth on Howler's leg with a grip that made him yell; then the half-breed dragged the dog away. That was enough for lesson No. 1. Now they hated each other; the bitter feud was on.

Next day a lesson was given again for both, and both learned other things: Way-atcha that that hole, the kennel, was a safe refuge; the cur, that the Coon could clutch as well as bite.

The third day came and the third lesson. Waiting for the cool of the evening, the hunter dropped the Coon into a bag, took down his gun, called the noisy dog, and made for the nearest stretch of woods, for the trailing and treeing of the Coon was to be the climax of the course of training.

Arrived at the timberland, Pete's first care was to tie the dog to a tree. Why? Certainly not out of consideration for the Coon, but for this: the Coon must be allowed to run and get out of sight, otherwise the dog does not try to follow it by track. Once he has to do this to find his prey, his own instinctive prompting makes him a trailer and he follows till he sights the quarry, then attacks, or if it trees, as is usual, he must ramp and rage against the trunk to let the hunter know the Coon is there. This is the training of a Coon dog; this was the plan of Indian Pete.

So the dog was chained to a sapling; the Coon was carried out of reach, and tumbled from the sack. Bewildered at first, but brave, he glared about, then seeing his tall enemy quite near he rushed open-mouthed at him. The half-breed ran away in some alarm, but laughing. The dog rushed at the Coon till the chain brought him up with a jerk, and now the Coon was free from all attack, was free to run. And then how he ran! With the quick instinct of a hunted race, he dashed away behind a tree to get out of sight, and, zig-zagging, bounded off, seeking the thickest cover, running as he never had run before.

Back came the half-breed to release the dog. Tight as a guy-rope was the chain that held that crazy, raging cur, so tight the chain that he could not get the little slack he needed to unhook the snap. Cursing the dog, jerking him back again and again, he fumbled to unhook the snap; and as he jerked and shouted, the dog jerked more and barked, so made it harder. Two or three minutes indeed he struggled to release the chain, and then he had to catch and hold the dog so as to free him by slipping his collar. Away went the dog to the place where last he saw the Coon.

But the victim was gone; those precious three minutes meant so much, and responsive to the hunter's 'sic him', 'sic him' the dog raced around. His nostrils found the trail, instinctively he yelped, then followed it, at every bound a yelp. Then he lost it, came back, found it again, and yelped, and slowly followed, for if he went too fast he lost it. And Pete ran, too, shouting encouragement, for all of this was in the plan. The Coon no doubt was running off, but soon the dog would find him, and then—oh, it never fails—the Coon climbs up the easiest tree, which means a small one always; the dog by yapping down below would guide the man, who coming up would shoot the Coon, which falling disabled would be worried by the dog, who thus has learned his part for future cooning, and thenceforth flushed with victory be even keener than his master for the chase.

Yes, that was the plan; it had often worked before, and did so now, but for one mishap. Way-atcha did not climb a slender tree. As soon as he was far away, thanks to that fumbled chain, and heard the raging of the two behind, he climbed the sort of tree that in his memory had been most a thing of safety to him. The big hollow maple was the haven of his youth, and up the biggest tree in all the woods he clambered now.

His foes came on; the dog was learning fast, was sticking to the trail. His master followed till they reached the mighty sycamore, and 'Here,' said Howler, 'we have treed him!' What the half-breed said we need not hear. He had brought his rifle, yes, but no axe. The Coon was safe in some great cavernous limb, for nowhere could they see him, and the tree could not be climbed by man. The night came down and Pete with his yapping dog went home defeated.

So luck was with Way-atcha, luck and the influence of his early days, that built in with his nature the secret of his race: this is their true abiding place—the hollow tree. The slender second growth most often near is a temptation and a snare, but the huge hollow trunk is a strong fortress and a sure salvation.

The Dog that Bit People

Probably no one man should have as many dogs in his life as I have had, but there was more pleasure than distress in them for me except in the case of an Airedale named Muggs. He gave me more trouble than all the other fifty-four or -five put together, although my moment of keenest embarrassment was the time a Scotch terrier named Jeannie, who had just had six puppies in the clothes closet of a fourth floor apartment in New York, had the unexpected seventh and last at the corner of Eleventh Street and Fifth Avenue during a walk she had insisted on taking. Then, too, there was the prize winning French poodle, a great big black poodle—none of your little, untroublesome white miniatures— who got sick riding in the rumble seat of a car with me on her way to the Greenwich Dog Show. She had a red rubber bib tucked around her throat and, since a rain storm came up when we were half way through the Bronx, I had to hold over her a small green umbrella, really more of a parasol. The rain beat down fearfully and suddenly the driver of the car drove into a big garage, filled with mechanics. It happened so quickly that I forgot to put the umbrella down and I will always remember, with sickening distress, the look of incredulity mixed with hatred that came over the face of the particular hardened garage man that came over to see what we wanted, when he took a look at me and the poodle. All garage men, and people of that intolerant stripe, hate poodles with their curious haircut, especially the pom-poms that you got to leave on their hips if you expect the dogs to win a prize.

But the Airedale, as I have said, was the worst of all my dogs. He really wasn't my dog, as a matter of fact: I came home from a vacation one summer to find that my brother Roy had bought him while I was away. A big, burly, choleric dog, he always acted as if he thought I wasn't one of the family. There was a slight advantage in being one of the family, for he didn't bite the family as often as he bit strangers. Still, in the years that we had him he bit everybody but mother, and he made a pass at her once but missed. That was during the month when we suddenly had mice, and Muggs refused to do anything about them. Nobody ever had mice exactly like the mice we had that month. They acted like pet mice, almost like mice somebody had trained. They were so friendly that one night when mother entertained at dinner the Friraliras, a club she and my father had belonged to for twenty years, she put down a lot of little dishes with food in them on the pantry floor so that the mice would be satisfied with that and wouldn't come into the dining room. Muggs stayed out in the pantry with the mice, lying on the floor, growling to himself—not at the mice, but about all the people in the next room that he would have liked to get at. Mother slipped out into the pantry once to see how everything was going. Everything was going fine. It made her so mad to see Muggs lying there, oblivious of the mice—they came running up to her—that she slapped him and he slashed at her, but didn't make it. He was sorry immediately, mother said. He was always sorry, she said, after he bit someone, but we could not understand how she figured this out. He didn't act sorry.

Mother used to send a box of candy every Christmas to the people the Airedale bit. The list finally contained forty or more names. Nobody could understand why we didn't get rid of the dog. I didn't understand it very well myself, but we didn't get rid of him. I think that one or two people tried to poison Muggs—he acted poisoned once in a while—and old Major Moberly fired at him once with his service revolver near the Seneca Hotel in East Broad Street—but Muggs lived to be almost eleven years old and even when he could hardly get around he bit a Congressman who had called to see my father on business. My mother had never liked the Congressman—she said the signs of his horoscope showed he couldn't be trusted (he was Saturn with the moon in Virgo)—but she sent him a box of candy that Christmas. He sent it right back, probably because he suspected it was trick candy. Mother persuaded herself it was all for the best that the dog had bitten him, even though father lost an important business association because of it. 'I wouldn't be associated with such a man,' mother said, 'Muggs could read him like a book.'

We used to take turns feeding Muggs to be on his good side, but that didn't always work. He was never in a very good humour, even after a meal. Nobody knew exactly what was the matter with him, but whatever it was it made him irascible, especially in the mornings. Roy never felt very well in the morning, either, especially before breakfast, and once when he came downstairs and found that Muggs had moodily chewed up the morning paper he hit him in the face with a grapefruit and then jumped up on the dining-room table, scattering dishes and silverware and spilling the coffee. Muggs' first free leap carried him all the way across the table and into a brass fire screen in front of the gas grate but he was back on his feet in a moment and in the end he got Roy and gave him a pretty vicious bite in the leg. Then he was all over it; he never bit anyone more than once at a time. Mother always mentioned that as an argument in his favour; she said he had a quick temper but that he didn't hold a grudge. She was forever defending him. I think she liked him because he wasn't well. 'He's not strong,' she would say, pityingly, but that was inaccurate; he may not have been well but he was terribly strong.

One time my mother went to the Chittenden Hotel to call on a woman mental healer who was lecturing in Columbus on the subject of 'Harmonious Vibrations'. She wanted to find out if it was possible to get harmonious vibrations into a dog. 'He's a large tan-coloured Airedale,' mother explained. The woman said that she had never treated a dog but she advised my mother to hold the thought that he did not bite and would not bite. Mother was holding the thought the very next morning when Muggs got the iceman but she blamed that slip-up on the iceman. 'If you didn't think he would bite you, he wouldn't,' mother told him. He stomped out of the house in a terrible jangle of vibrations.

One morning when Muggs bit me slightly, more or less in passing, I reached down and grabbed his short stumpy tail and hoisted him into the air. It was a foolhardy thing to do and the last time I saw my mother, about six months ago, she said she didn't know what possessed me. I don't either, except that I was pretty mad. As long as I held the dog off the floor by his tail he couldn't get at me, but he twisted and jerked so, snarling all the time, that I realized I couldn't hold him that way very long. I carried him to the kitchen and flung him on to the floor and shut the door on him just as he crashed against it. But I forgot about the back-stairs. Muggs went up the backstairs and down the frontstairs and had me cornered in the living room. I managed to get up on to the mantelpiece above the fireplace, but it gave way and came down with a tremendous crash throwing a large marble clock, several vases, and myself heavily to the floor. Muggs was so alarmed by the racket that when I picked myself up he had disappeared. We couldn't find him anywhere, although we whistled and shouted, until old Mrs Detweiler called after dinner that night. Muggs had bitten her once, in the leg, and she came into the living room only after we assured her that Muggs had run away. She had just seated herself when, with a great growling and scratching of claws, Muggs emerged from under a davenport where he had been quietly hiding all the time, and bit her again. Mother examined the bite and put arnica on it and told Mrs Detweiler that it was only a bruise. 'He just bumped you,' she said. But Mrs Detweiler left the house in a nasty state of mind.

Lots of people reported our Airedale to the police but my father held a municipal office at the time and was on friendly terms with the police. Even so, the cops had been out a couple of times—once when Muggs bit Mrs Rufus Sturtevant and again when he bit Lieutenant-Governor Malloy—but mother told them that it hadn't been Muggs' fault but the fault of the people who were bitten. 'When he starts for them, they scream,' she explained, 'and that excites him.' The cops suggested that it might be a good idea to tie the dog up, but mother said that it mortified him to be tied up and that he wouldn't eat when he was tied up.

Muggs at his meals was an unusual sight. Because of the fact that if you reached towards the floor he would bite you, we usually put his food plate on top of an old kitchen table with a bench alongside the table. Muggs would stand on the bench and eat. I remember that my mother's Uncle Horatio, who boasted that he was the third man up Missionary Ridge, was splutteringly indignant when he found out that we fed the dog on a table because we were afraid to put his plate on the floor. He said he wasn't afraid of any dog that ever lived and that he would put the dog's plate on the floor if we would give it to him. Roy said that if Uncle Horatio had fed Muggs on the ground just before the battle he would have been the first man up Missionary Ridge. Uncle Horatio was furious. 'Bring him in! Bring him in now!' he shouted. 'I'll feed the —— on the floor!' Roy was all for giving him a chance, but my father wouldn't hear of it. He said that Muggs had already been fed. 'I'll feed him again!' bawled Uncle Horatio. We had quite a time quieting him.

In his last year Muggs used to spend practically all of his time outdoors. He didn't like to stay in the house for some reason or other—perhaps it held too many unpleasant memories for him. Anyway, it was hard to get him to come in and as a result the garbage man, the iceman, and the laundryman wouldn't come near the house. We had to haul the garbage down to the corner, take the laundry out and bring it back, and meet the iceman a block from home. After this had gone on for some time we hit on an ingenious arrangement for getting the dog in the house so that we could lock him up while the gas meter was read, and so on. Muggs was afraid of only one thing, an electrical storm. Thunder and lightning frightened him out of his senses (I think he thought a storm had broken the day the mantelpiece fell). He would rush into the house and hide under a bed or in a clothes closet. So we fixed up a thunder machine out of a long narrow piece of sheet iron with a wooden handle on one end. Mother would shake this vigorously when she wanted to get Muggs into the house. It made an excellent imitation of thunder, but I suppose it was the most roundabout system for running a household that was ever devised. It took a lot out of mother.

A few months before Muggs died, he got to 'seeing things'. He would rise slowly from the floor, growling low, and stalk stiff-legged and menacing towards nothing at all. Sometimes the Thing would be just a little to the right or left of a visitor. Once a Fuller Brush salesman got hysterics. Muggs came wandering into the room like Hamlet following his father's ghost. His eyes were fixed on a spot just to the left of the Fuller Brush man, who stood it until Muggs was about three slow, creeping paces from him. Then he shouted. Muggs wavered on past him into the hallway grumbling to himself but the Fuller man went on shouting. I think mother had to throw a pan of cold water on him before he stopped. That was the way she used to stop us boys when we got into fights.

Muggs died quite suddenly one night. Mother wanted to bury him in the family lot under a marble stone with some such inscription as 'Flights of angels sing thee to thy rest' but we persuaded her it was against the law. In the end we just put up a smooth board above his grave along a lonely road. On the board I wrote with an indelible pencil 'Cave Canem'. Mother was quite pleased with the simple classic dignity of the old Latin epitaph.

Rudyard Kipling

The Miracle of Purun Bhagat

There was once a man in India who was Prime Minister of one of the semi-independent native States in the north-western part of the country. He was a Brahmin, so high-caste that caste ceased to have any particular meaning for him; and his father had been an important official in the gay-coloured tag-rag and bobtail of an old-fashioned Hindu Court. But as Purun Dass grew up he felt that the old order of things was changing, and that if any one wished to get on in the world he must stand well with the English, and imitate all that the English believed to be good. At the same time a native official must keep his own master's favour. This was a difficult game, but the quiet, close-mouthed young Brahmin, helped by a good English education at a Bombay University, played it coolly, and rose, step by step, to be Prime Minister of the kingdom. That is to say, he held more real power than his master, the Maharajah.

When the old king—who was suspicious of the English, their railways and telegraphs—died, Purun Dass stood high with his young successor, who had been tutored by an Englishman; and between them, though he always took care that his master should have the credit, they established schools for little girls, made roads, and started State dispensaries and shows of agricultural imple- ments, and published a yearly blue-book on the 'Moral and Material Progress of the State', and the Foreign Office and the Government of India were delighted. Very few native States take up English progress altogether, for they will not believe, as Purun Dass showed he did, that what was good for the Englishman must be twice as good for the Asiatic. The Prime Minister became the honoured friend of Viceroys, and Governors, and Lieutenant-Gov- ernors, and medical missionaries, and common missionaries, and hard-riding English officers who came to shoot in the State pre- serves, as well as of whole hosts of tourists who travelled up and down India in the cold weather, showing how things ought to be managed. In his spare time he would endow scholarships for the study of medicine and manufactures on strictly English lines, and write letters to the *Pioneer*, the greatest Indian daily paper, explaining his master's aims and objects.

At last he went to England on a visit, and had to pay enormous sums to the priests when he came back; for even so high-caste a Brahmin as Purun Dass lost caste by crossing the black sea. In London he met and talked with every one worth knowing—men whose names go all over the world—and saw a great deal more than he said. He was given honorary degrees by learned universities, and he made speeches and talked of Hindu social reform to English ladies in evening dress, till all London cried, 'This is the most fascinating man we have ever met at dinner since cloths were first laid.'

When he returned to India there was a blaze of glory, for the Viceroy himself made a special visit to confer upon the Maharajah the Grand Cross of the Star of India—all diamonds and ribbons and enamel; and at the same ceremony, while the cannon boomed, Purun Dass was made a Knight Commander of the Order of the Indian Empire; so that his name stood Sir Purun Dass, K.C.I.E.

That evening, at dinner in the big Viceregal tent, he stood up with the badge and the collar of the Order on his breast, and replying to the toast of his master's health, made a speech few Englishmen could have bettered.

Next month, when the city had returned to its sun-baked quiet, he did a thing no Englishman would have dreamed of doing; for, so far as the world's affairs went, he died. The jewelled order of his knighthood went back to the Indian Government, and a new Prime Minister was appointed to the charge of affairs, and a great game of General Post began in all the subordinate appointments. The priests knew what had happened, and the people guessed; but India is the one place in the world where a man can do as he pleases and nobody asks why; and the fact that Dewan Sir Purun Dass, K.C.I.E., had resigned position, palace, and power, and taken up the begging-bowl and ochre-coloured dress of a Sunnyasi, or holy man, was considered nothing extraordinary. He had been, as the Old Law recommends, twenty years a youth, twenty years a fighter—though he had never carried a weapon in his life—and twenty years head of a household. He had used his wealth and his power for what he knew both to be worth; he had taken honour when it came his way; he had seen men and cities far and near, and men and cities had stood up and honoured him. Now he would let these things go, as a man drops the cloak he no longer needs.

Behind him, as he walked through the city gates, an antelope skin and brass-handled crutch under his arm, and a begging-bowl of polished brown *coco-de-mer* in his hand, barefoot, alone, with eyes cast on the ground—behind him they were firing salutes from the bastions in honour of his happy successor. Purun Dass nodded. All that life was ended; and he bore it no more ill-will or good-will than a man bears to a colourless dream of the night. He was a Sunnyasi—a houseless, wandering mendicant, depending on his neighbours for his daily bread; and so long as there is a morsel to divide in India, neither priest nor beggar starves. He had never in his life tasted meat, and very seldom eaten even fish. A five-pound note would have covered his personal expenses for food through any one of the many years in which he had been absolute master of millions of money. Even when he was being lionized in London he had held before him his dream of peace and quiet—the long, white, dusty Indian road, printed all over with bare feet, the incessant, slow-moving traffic, and the sharp-smelling wood smoke curling up under the fig-trees in the twilight, where the wayfarers sit at their evening meal.

When the time came to make that dream true the Prime Minister took the proper steps, and in three days you might more easily have found a bubble in the trough of the long Atlantic seas than Purun Dass among the roving, gathering, separating millions of India.

At night his antelope skin was spread where the darkness overtook him—sometimes in a Sunnyasi monastery by the roadside; sometimes by a mud-pillar shrine of Kala Pir, where the Jogis, who are another misty division of holy men, would receive him as they do those who know what castes and visions are worth; sometimes on the outskirts of a little Hindu village, where the children would steal up with the food their parents had prepared; and sometimes on the pitch of the bare grazing-grounds, where the flame of his stick fire waked the drowsy camels. It was all one to Purun Dass—or Purun Bhagat, as he called himself now. Earth, people, and food were all one. But unconsciously his feet drew him away northward and eastward; from the south to Rohtak; from Rohtak to Kurnool; from Kurnool to ruined Samanah, and then up-stream along the dried bed of the Gugger river that fills only when the rain falls in the hills, till one day he saw the far line of the great Himalayas.

Then Purun Bhagat smiled, for he remembered that his mother was of Rajput Brahmin birth, from Kulu way—a Hill-woman, always home-sick for the snows—and that the least touch of Hill blood draws a man in the end back to where he belongs.

'Yonder,' said Purun Bhagat, breasting the lower slopes of the

Sewaliks, where the cacti stand up like seven-branched candle-sticks—'yonder I shall sit down and get knowledge'; and the cool wind of the Himalayas whistled about his ears as he trod the road that led to Simla.

The last time he had come that way it had been in state, with a clattering cavalry escort, to visit the gentlest and most affable of Viceroys; and the two had talked together about mutual friends in London, and what the Indian common folk really thought of things. This time Purun Bhagat paid no calls, but leaned on the rail of the Mall, watching that glorious view of the Plains spread out forty miles below, till a native Mohammedan policeman told him he was obstructing traffic; and Purun Bhagat salaamed reverently to the Law, because he knew the value of it, and was seeking for a Law of his own. Then he moved on, and slept that night in an empty hut at Chota Simla, which looks like the very last end of the earth, but it was only the beginning of his journey.

He followed the Himalaya–Thibet road, the little ten-foot track that is blasted out of solid rock, or strutted out on timbers over gulfs a thousand feet deep; that dips into warm, wet, shut-in valleys, and climbs out across bare, grassy hill-shoulders where the sun strikes like a burning-glass; or turns through dripping, dark forests where the tree-ferns dress the trunks from head to heel, and the pheasant calls to his mate. And he met Thibetan herdsmen with their dogs and flocks of sheep, each sheep with a little bag of borax on his back, and wandering wood-cutters, and cloaked and blanketed Lamas from Thibet, coming into India on pilgrim-age, and envoys of little solitary Hill-states, posting furiously on ring-streaked and piebald ponies, or the cavalcade of a Rajah paying a visit; or else for a long, clear day he would see nothing more than a black bear grunting and rooting below in the valley. When he first started, the roar of the world he had left still rang in his ears, as the roar of a tunnel rings long after the train has passed through; but when he had put the Mutteeanee Pass behind him that was all done, and Purun Bhagat was alone with himself, walking, wondering, and thinking, his eyes on the ground, and his thoughts with the clouds.

One evening he crossed the highest pass he had met till then— it had been a two-days' climb—and came out on a line of snow-peaks that banded all the horizon—mountains from 15 000 to 20 000 feet high, looking almost near enough to hit with a stone, though they were fifty or sixty miles away. The pass was crowned with dense, dark forest—deodar, walnut, wild cherry, wild olive, and wild pear, but mostly deodar, which is the Himalayan cedar; and under the shadow of the deodars stood a deserted shrine to Kali—who is Durga, who is Sitala, who is sometimes worshipped against the smallpox.

Purun Dass swept the stone floor clean, smiled at the grinning statue, made himself a little mud fireplace at the back of the shrine, spread his antelope skin on a bed of fresh pine-needles, tucked his *bairagi*—his brass-handled crutch—under his armpit, and sat down to rest.

Immediately below him the hillside fell away, clean and cleared for 1500 feet, where a little village of stone-walled houses, with roofs of beaten earth, clung to the steep tilt. All round it the tiny terraced fields lay out like aprons of patchwork on the knees of the mountain, and cows no bigger than beetles grazed between the smooth stone circles of the threshing-floors. Looking across the valley, the eye was deceived by the size of things, and could not at first realize that what seemed to be low scrub, on the opposite mountain-flank, was in truth a forest of 100-foot pines. Purun Bhagat saw an eagle sweep across the gigantic hollow, but the great bird dwindled to a dot ere it was half-way over. A few bands of scattered clouds strung up and down the valley, catching on a shoulder of the hills, or rising up and dying out when they were level with the head of the pass. And 'Here shall I find peace,' said Purun Bhagat.

Now, a Hill-man makes nothing of a few hundred feet up or down, and as soon as the villagers saw the smoke in the deserted shrine, the village priest climbed up the terraced hillside to welcome the stranger.

When he met Purun Bhagat's eyes—the eyes of a man used to control thousands—he bowed to the earth, took the begging-bowl without a word, and turned to the village, saying, 'We have at last a holy man. Never have I seen such a man. He is of the Plains—but pale-coloured—a Brahmin of the Brahmins.' Then all the housewives of the village said, 'Think you he will stay with us?' and each did her best to cook the most savoury meal for the Bhagat. Hill-food is very simple, but with buckwheat and Indian corn, and rice and red pepper, and little fish out of the stream in the valley, and honey from the flue-like hives built in the stone walls, and dried apricots, and turmeric, and wild ginger, and bannocks of flour, a devout woman can make good things, and it was a full bowl that the priest carried to the Bhagat. Was he going to stay? asked the priest. Would he need a *chela*—a disciple—to beg for him? Had he a blanket against the cold weather? Was the food good?

Purun Bhagat ate, and thanked the giver. It was in his mind to stay. That was sufficient, said the priest. Let the begging-bowl be placed outside the shrine, in the hollow made by those two twisted roots, and daily should the Bhagat be fed; for the village felt honoured that such a man—he looked timidly into the Bhagat's face—should tarry among them.

That day saw the end of Purun Bhagat's wanderings. He had come to the place appointed for him—the silence and the space. After this, time stopped, and he, sitting at the mouth of the shrine, could not tell whether he were alive or dead; a man with control of his limbs, or a part of the hills, and the clouds, and the shifting rain and sunlight. He would repeat a Name softly to himself a hundred hundred times, till, at each repetition, he seemed to move more and more out of his body, sweeping up to the doors of some tremendous discovery; but, just as the door was opening, his body would drag him back, and, with grief, he felt he was locked up again in the flesh and bones of Purun Bhagat.

Every morning the filled begging-bowl was laid silently in the crutch of the roots outside the shrine. Sometimes the priest brought it; sometimes a Ladakhi trader, lodging in the village, and anxious to get merit, trudged up the path; but, more often, it was the woman who had cooked the meal overnight; and she would murmur, hardly above her breath: 'Speak for me before the gods, Bhagat. Speak for such a one, the wife of so-and-so!' Now and then some bold child would be allowed the honour, and Purun Bhagat would hear him drop the bowl and run as fast as his little legs could carry him, but the Bhagat never came down to the village. It was laid out like a map at his feet. He could see the evening gatherings, held on the circle of the threshing-floors, because that was the only level ground; could see the wonderful unnamed green of the young rice, the indigo blues of the Indian corn, the dock-like patches of buckwheat, and, in its season, the red bloom of the amaranth, whose tiny seeds, being neither grain nor pulse, make a food that can be lawfully eaten by Hindus in time of fasts.

When the year turned, the roofs of the huts were all little squares of purest gold, for it was on the roofs that they laid out their cobs of the corn to dry. Hiving and harvest, rice-sowing and husking, passed before his eyes, all embroidered down there on the many-sided plots of fields, and he thought of them all, and wondered what they all led to at the long last.

Even in populated India a man cannot a day sit still before the wild things run over him as though he were a rock; and in that wilderness very soon the wild things, who knew Kali's Shrine well, came back to look at the intruder. The *langurs*, the big grey-whiskered monkeys of the Himalayas, were, naturally, the first, for they are alive with curiosity; and when they had upset the beg-ging-bowl, and rolled it round the floor, and tried their teeth on the brass-handled crutch, and made faces at the antelope skin, they decided that the human being who sat so still was harmless. At evening, they would leap down from the pines, and beg with their hands for things to eat, and then swing off in graceful curves. They liked the warmth of the fire, too, and huddled round it till Purun Bhagat had to push them aside to throw on more fuel; and in the morning, as often as not, he would find a furry ape sharing his blanket. All day long, one or other of the tribe would sit by his side, staring out at the snows, crooning and looking unspeakably wise and sorrowful.

After the monkeys came the *barasingh*, that big deer which is like our red deer, but stronger. He wished to rub off the velvet of his horns against the cold stones of Kali's statue, and stamped his feet when he saw the man at the shrine. But Purun Bhagat never moved, and, little by little the royal stag edged up and nuzzled his shoulder. Purun Bhagat slid one cool hand along the hot antlers, and the touch soothed the fretted beast, who bowed his head, and Purun Bhagat very softly rubbed and ravelled off the velvet. After-ward, the *barasingh* brought his doe and fawn—gentle things that mumbled on the holy man's blanket—or would come alone at night, his eyes green in the fire-flicker, to take his share of fresh walnuts. At last, the musk-deer, the shyest and almost the smallest of the deerlets, came, too, her big rabbity ears erect; even brindled, silent *mushick-nabha* must needs find out what the light in the shrine meant, and drop out her moose-like nose into Purun Bhagat's lap, coming and going with the shadows of the fire. Purun Bhagat called them all 'my brothers', and his low call of '*Bhai! Bhai!* ' would draw them from the forest at noon if they were within earshot. The Himalayan black bear, moody and suspicious—Sona, who has the V-shaped white mark under his chin—passed that way more than once; and since Bhagat showed no fear, Sona showed no anger, but watched him, and came closer, and begged a share of the caresses, and a dole of bread or wild berries. Often, in the still dawns, when the Bhagat would climb to the very crest of the pass to watch the red day walking along the peaks of the snows, he would find Sona shuffling and grunting at his heels, thrusting a curious fore-paw under fallen trunks, and bringing it away with a *whoof* of impatience; or his early steps would wake Sona where he lay curled up, and the great brute, rising erect, would think to fight, till he heard the Bhagat's voice and knew his best friend.

Nearly all hermits and holy men who live apart from the big cities have the reputation of being able to work miracles with the wild things, but all the miracle lies in keeping still, in never making a hasty movement, and, for a long time, at least, in never looking directly at a visitor. The villagers saw the outline of the *barasingh* stalking like a shadow through the dark forest behind the shrine; saw the *minaul*, the Himalayan pheasant, blazing in her best colours before Kali's statue; and the *langurs* on their haunches, inside, playing with the walnut shells. Some of the children, too, had heard Sona singing to himself, bear-fashion, behind the fallen rocks, and the Bhagat's reputation as miracle-worker stood firm.

Yet nothing was farther from his mind than miracles. He believed that all things were one big Miracle, and when a man knows that much he knows something to go upon. He knew for a certainty that there was nothing great and nothing little in this world: and day and night he strove to think out his way into the heart of things, back to the place whence his soul had come.

So thinking, his untrimmed hair fell down about his shoulders, the stone slab at the side of the antelope skin was dented into a little hole by the foot of his brass-handled crutch, and the place between the tree-trunks, where the begging-bowl rested day after day, sunk and wore into a hollow almost as smooth as the brown shell itself; and each beast knew his exact place at the fire. The fields changed their colours with the seasons; the threshing-floors filled and emptied, and filled again and again; and again and again, when winter came, the *langurs* frisked among the branches feathered with light snow, till the mother-monkeys brought their sad-eyed little babies up from the warmer valleys with the spring. There were few changes in the village. The priest was older, and many of the little children who used to come with the begging-dish sent their own children now; and when you asked of the villagers how long their holy man had lived in Kali's Shrine at the head of the pass, they answered, 'Always.'

Then came such summer rains as had not been known in the Hills for many seasons. Through three good months the valley was wrapped in cloud and soaking mist—steady, unrelenting downfall, breaking off into thunder-shower after thunder-shower. Kali's Shrine stood above the clouds, for the most part, and there was a whole month in which the Bhagat never caught a glimpse of his village. It was packed away under a white floor of cloud that swayed and shifted and rolled on itself and bulged upward, but never broke from its piers—the streaming flanks of the valley.

All that time he heard nothing but the sound of a million little waters, overhead from the trees, and underfoot along the ground, soaking through the pine-needles, dripping from the tongues of draggled fern, and spouting in newly-torn muddy channels down the slopes. Then the sun came out, and drew forth the good incense of the deodars and the rhododendrons, and that far-off, clean smell which the Hill people call 'the smell of the snows'. The hot sunshine lasted for a week, and then the rains gathered together for their last downpour, and the water fell in sheets that flayed off the skin of the ground and leaped back in mud. Purun Bhagat heaped his fire high that night, for he was sure his brothers would need warmth; but never a beast came to the shrine, though he called and called till he dropped asleep, wondering what had happened in the woods.

It was in the black heart of the night, the rain drumming like a thousand drums, that he was roused by a plucking at his blanket, and, stretching out, felt the little hand of a *langur*. 'It is better here than in the trees,' he said sleepily, loosening a fold of blanket; 'take it and be warm.' The monkey caught his hand and pulled hard. 'Is it food, then?' said Purun Bhagat. 'Wait awhile, and I will pre-pare some.' As he kneeled to throw fuel on the fire the *langur* ran to the door of the shrine, crooned, and ran back again, plucking at the man's knee.

'What is it? What is thy trouble, Brother?' said Purun Bhagat, for the *langur's* eyes were full of things that he could not tell. 'Unless one of thy caste be in a trap—and none set traps here—I will not go into that weather. Look, Brother, even the *barasingh* comes for shelter!'

The deer's antlers clashed as he strode into the shrine, clashed against the grinning statue of Kali. He lowered them in Purun Bha-gat's direction and stamped uneasily, hissing through his half-shut nostrils.

'Hai! Hai! Hai!' said the Bhagat, snapping his fingers. 'Is *this* payment for a night's lodging?' But the deer pushed him towards the door, and as he did so Purun Bhagat heard the sound of some-thing opening with a sigh, and saw two slabs of the floor draw away from each other, while the sticky earth below smacked its lips.

'Now I see,' said Purun Bhagat. 'No blame to my brothers that they did not sit by the fire tonight. The mountain is falling. And yet—why should I go?' His eye fell on the empty begging-bowl, and his face changed. 'They have given me good food daily since—since I came, and, if I am not swift, tomorrow there will not be one mouth in the valley. Indeed, I must go and warn them below. Back there, Brother! Let me get to the fire.'

The *barasingh* backed unwillingly as Purun Bhagat drove a pine torch deep into the flame, twirling it till it was well lit. 'Ah! ye came to warn me,' he said, rising. 'Better than that we shall do; better than that. Out, now, and lend me thy neck, Brother, for I have but two feet.'

He clutched the bristling withers of the *barasingh* with his right hand, held the torch away with his left, and stepped out of the shrine into the desperate night. There was no breath of wind, but the rain nearly drowned the flare as the great deer hurried down the slope, sliding on his haunches. As soon as they were clear of the forest more of the Bhagat's brothers joined them. He heard, though he could not see, the *langurs* pressing about him, and behind them the uhh! uhh! of Sona. The rain matted his long white hair into ropes; the water splashed beneath his bare feet, and his yellow robe clung to his frail old body, but he stepped down steadily, leaning against the *barasingh*. He was no longer a holy man, but Sir Purun Dass, K.C.I.E., Prime Minister of no small State, a man accustomed to command, going out to save life. Down the steep, plashy path they poured all together, the Bhagat and his brothers, down and down till the deer's feet clicked and stumbled on the wall of a threshing-floor, and he snorted because he smelt Man. Now they were at the head of the one crooked village street, and the Bhagat beat with his crutch on the barred windows of the black-smith's house, as his torch blazed up in the shelter of the eaves. 'Up and out!' cried Purun Bhagat; and he did not know his own voice, for it was years since he had spoken aloud to a man. 'The hill falls! The hill is falling! Up and out, oh, you within!'

'It is our Bhagat,' said the blacksmith's wife. 'He stands among his beasts. Gather the little ones and give the call.'

It ran from house to house, while the beasts, cramped in the narrow way, surged and huddled round the Bhagat, and Sona puffed impatiently.

The people hurried into the street—they were no more than seventy souls all told—and in the glare of the torches they saw their Bhagat holding back the terrified *barasingh*, while the monkeys plucked piteously at his skirts, and Sona sat on his haunches and roared.

'Across the valley and up the next hill!' shouted Purun Bhagat. 'Leave none behind! We follow!'

Then the people ran as only Hill folk can run, for they knew that in a landslide you must climb for the highest ground across the valley. They fled, splashing through the little river at the bottom, and panted up the terraced fields on the far side, while the Bhagat and his brethren followed. Up and up the opposite mountain they climbed, calling to each other by name—the roll-call of the village—and at their heels toiled the big *barasingh*, weighted by the failing strength of Purun Bhagat. At last the deer stopped in the shadow of a deep pine-wood, 500 feet up the hillside. His instinct, that had warned him of the coming slide, told him he would be safe here.

Purun Bhagat dropped fainting by his side, for the chill of the rain and that fierce climb were killing him; but first he called to the scattered torches ahead, 'Stay and count your numbers'; then, whispering to the deer as he saw the lights gather in a cluster: 'Stay with me, Brother. Stay—till—I—go!'

There was a sigh in the air that grew to a mutter, and a mutter that grew to a roar, and a roar that passed all sense of hearing, and the hillside on which the villagers stood was hit in the darkness, and rocked to the blow. Then a note as steady, deep, and true as the deep C of the organ drowned everything for perhaps five minutes, while the very roots of the pines quivered to it. It died away, and the sound of the rain falling on miles of hard ground and grass changed to the muffled drum of water on soft earth. That told its own tale.

Never a villager—not even the priest—was bold enough to speak to the Bhagat who had saved their lives. They crouched under the pines and waited till the day. When it came they looked across the valley and saw that what had been forest, and terraced field, and track-threaded grazing-ground was one raw, red, fan-shaped smear, with a few trees flung head-down on the scarp. That red ran high up the hill of their refuge, damming back the little river, which had begun to spread into a brick-coloured lake. Of the village, of the road to the shrine, of the shrine itself, and the forest behind, there was no trace. For one mile in width and 2000 feet in sheer depth the mountain-side had come away bodily, planed clean from head to heel.

And the villagers, one by one, crept through the wood to pray before their Bhagat. They saw the *barasingh* standing over him, who fled when they came near, and they heard the *langurs* wailing in the branches, and Sona moaning up the hill; but their Bhagat was dead, sitting cross-legged, his back against a tree, his crutch under his armpit, and his face turned to the north-east.

The priest said: 'Behold a miracle after a miracle, for in this very attitude must all Sunnyasis be buried! Therefore where he now is we will build the temple to our holy man.'

They built the temple before a year was ended—a little stone-and-earth shrine—and they called the hill the Bhagat's Hill, and they worship there with lights and flowers and offerings to this day. But they do not know that the saint of their worship is the late Sir Purun Dass, K.C.I.E., D.C.L., Ph.D., etc., once Prime Minister of the progressive and enlightened State of Mohiniwala, and honorary or corresponding member of more learned and scientific societies than will ever do any good in this world or the next.

Saki

Tobermory

It was a chill, rain-washed afternoon of a late August day, that indefinite season when partridges are still in security or cold storage, and there is nothing to hunt—unless one is bounded on the north by the Bristol Channel, in which case one may lawfully gallop after fat red stags. Lady Blemley's house-party was not bounded on the north by the Bristol Channel, hence there was a full gathering of her guests round the tea table on this particular afternoon. And, in spite of the blankness of the season and the triteness of the occasion, there was no trace in the company of that fatigued restlessness which means a dread of the pianola and a subdued hankering for auction bridge. The undisguised open-mouthed attention of the entire party was fixed on the homely negative personality of Mr Cornelius Appin. Of all her guests, he was the one who had come to Lady Blemley with the vaguest reputation. Someone had said he was 'clever', and he had got his invitation in the moderate expectation, on the part of his hostess, that some portion at least of his cleverness would be contributed to the general entertainment. Until tea time that day she had been unable to discover in what direction, if any, his cleverness lay. He was neither a wit nor a croquet champion, a hypnotic force nor a begetter of amateur theatricals. Neither did his exterior suggest the sort of man in whom women are willing to pardon a generous measure of mental deficiency. He had subsided into mere Mr Appin, and the Cornelius seemed a piece of transparent baptismal bluff. And now he was claiming to have launched on the world a discovery beside which the invention of gunpowder, of the printing-press, and of steam locomotion were inconsiderable trifles. Science had made bewildering strides in many directions during recent decades but this thing seemed to belong to the domain of miracle rather than to scientific achievement.

'And do you really ask us to believe,' Sir Wilfrid was saying, 'that you have discovered a means for instructing animals in the art of human speech, and that dear old Tobermory has proved your first successful pupil?'

'It is a problem at which I have worked for the last seventeen years,' said Mr Appin, 'but only during the last eight or nine months have I been rewarded with glimmerings of success. Of course I have experimented with thousands of animals, but latterly only with cats, those wonderful creatures which have assimilated themselves so marvellously with our civilization while retaining all their highly developed feral instincts. Here and there among cats one comes across an outstanding superior intellect, just as one does among the ruck of human beings, and when I made the acquaintance of Tobermory a week ago I saw at once that I was in contact with a "Beyond-cat" of extraordinary intelligence. I had gone far along the road to success in recent experiments; with Tobermory, as you call him, I have reached the goal.'

Mr Appin concluded his remarkable statement in a voice which he strove to divest of a triumphant inflection. No one said 'Rats', though Clovis's lips moved in a monosyllabic contortion which probably invoked those rodents of disbelief.

'And do you mean to say,' asked Miss Resker, after a slight pause, 'that you have taught Tobermory to say and understand easy sentences of one syllable?'

'My dear Miss Resker,' said the wonder-worker patiently, 'one teaches little children and savages and backward adults in that piecemeal fashion; when one has once solved the problem of making a beginning with an animal of highly developed intelligence one has no need for those halting methods. Tobermory can speak our language with perfect correctness.'

This time Clovis very distinctly said, 'Beyond-rats!' Sir Wilfrid was more polite, but equally sceptical.

'Hadn't we better have the cat in and judge for ourselves?' suggested Lady Blemley.

Sir Wilfrid went in search of the animal, and the company settled themselves down to the languid expectation of witnessing some more or less adroit drawing-room ventriloquism.

In a minute Sir Wilfrid was back in the room, his face white beneath its tan and his eyes dilated with excitement.

'By Gad, it's true!'

His agitation was unmistakably genuine, and his hearers started forward in a thrill of awakened interest.

Collapsing into an armchair he continued breathlessly: 'I found him dozing in the smoking-room, and called out to him to come for his tea. He blinked at me in his usual way, and I said, "Come on, Toby; don't keep us waiting"; and, by Gad! he drawled out in a most horribly natural voice that he'd come when he dashed well pleased! I nearly jumped out of my skin!'

Appin had preached to absolutely incredulous hearers; Sir Wilfrid's statement carried instant conviction. A Babel-like chorus of startled exclamation arose, amid which the scientist sat mutely enjoying the first fruit of his stupendous discovery.

In the midst of the clamour Tobermory entered the room and made his way with velvet tread and studied unconcern across to the group seated round the tea table.

A sudden hush of awkwardness and constraint fell on the company. Somehow there seemed an element of embarrassment in addressing on equal terms a domestic cat of acknowledged mental ability.

'Will you have some milk, Tobermory?' asked Lady Blemley in a rather strained voice.

'I don't mind if I do,' was the response, couched in a tone of even indifference. A shiver of suppressed excitement went through the listeners, and Lady Blemley might be excused for pouring out the saucerful of milk rather unsteadily.

'I'm afraid I've spilt a good deal of it,' she said apologetically.

'After all, it's not my Axminster,' was Tobermory's rejoinder.

Another silence fell on the group, and then Miss Resker, in her best district-visitor manner, asked if the human language had been difficult to learn. Tobermory looked squarely at her for a moment and then fixed his gaze serenely on the middle distance. It was obvious that boring questions lay outside his scheme of life.

'What do you think of human intelligence?' asked Mavis Pellington lamely.

'Of whose intelligence in particular?' asked Tobermory coldly.

'Oh, well, mine for instance,' said Mavis, with a feeble laugh.

'You put me in an embarrassing position,' said Tobermory, whose tone and attitude certainly did not suggest a shred of embarrassment. 'When your inclusion in this house-party was suggested Sir Wilfrid protested that you were the most brainless woman of his acquaintance, and that there was a wide distinction between hospitality and the care of the feeble-minded. Lady Blemley replied that your lack of brain-power was the precise quality which had earned you your invitation, as you were the only person she could think of who might be idiotic enough to buy their old car. You know, the one they call "The Envy of Sisyphus", because it goes quite nicely uphill if you push it.'

Lady Blemley's protestations would have had greater effect if she had not casually suggested to Mavis only that morning that the car in question would be just the thing for her down at her Devonshire home.

Major Barfield plunged in heavily to effect a diversion.

'How about your carryings-on with the tortoise-shell puss up at the stables, eh?'

The moment he had said it everyone realized the blunder.

'One does not usually discuss these matters in public,' said Tobermory frigidly. 'From a slight observation of your ways since you've been in this house I should imagine you'd find it inconvenient if I were to shift the conversation on to your own little affairs.'

The panic which ensued was not confined to the Major.

'Would you like to go and see if cook has got your dinner ready?' suggested Lady Blemley hurriedly, affecting to ignore the fact that it wanted at least two hours to Tobermory's dinner time.

'Thanks,' said Tobermory, 'not quite so soon after my tea. I don't want to die of indigestion.'

'Cats have nine lives, you know,' said Sir Wilfrid heartily.

'Possibly,' answered Tobermory; 'but only one liver.'

'Adelaide!' said Mrs Cornett, 'do you mean to encourage that cat to go out and gossip about us in the servants' hall?'

The panic had indeed become general. A narrow ornamental balustrade ran in front of most of the bedroom windows at the Towers, and it was recalled with dismay that this had formed a favourite promenade for Tobermory at all hours, when he could watch the pigeons—and heaven knew what else besides. If he intended to become reminiscent in his present outspoken strain the effect would be something more than disconcerting. Mrs Cornett, who spent much time at her toilet table, and whose complexion was reputed to be of a nomadic though punctual disposition, looked as ill at ease as the Major. Miss Scrawen, who wrote fiercely sensuous poetry and led a blameless life, merely displayed irritation; if you are methodical and virtuous in private you don't necessarily want everyone to know it. Bertie van Tahn, who was so depraved at seventeen that he had long ago given up trying to be any worse, turned a dull shade of gardenia white, but he did not commit the error of dashing out of the room like Odo Finsberry, a young gentleman who was understood to be reading for the Church and who was possibly disturbed at the thought of scandals he might hear concerning other people. Clovis had the presence of mind to maintain a composed exterior; privately he was calculating how long it would take to procure a box of fancy mice through the agency of the *Exchange and Mart* as a species of hush-money.

Even in a delicate situation like the present, Agnes Resker could not endure to remain too long in the background.

'Why did I ever come down here?' she asked dramatically.

Tobermory immediately accepted the opening.

'Judging by what you said to Mrs Cornett on the croquet-lawn yesterday, you were out for food. You described the Blemleys as the dullest people to stay with that you knew, but said they were clever enough to employ a first-rate cook; otherwise they'd find it difficult to get anyone to come down a second time.'

'There's not a word of truth in it! I appeal to Mrs Cornett—' exclaimed the discomfited Agnes.

'Mrs Cornett repeated your remark afterwards to Bertie van Tahn,' continued Tobermory, 'and said, "That woman is a regular Hunger Marcher; she'd go anywhere for four square meals a day," and Bertie van Tahn said—'

At this point the chronicle mercifully ceased. Tobermory had caught a glimpse of the big yellow Tom from the Rectory working his way through the shrubbery towards the stable wing. In a flash he had vanished through the open French window.

With the disappearance of his too brilliant pupil Cornelius Appin found himself beset by a hurricane of bitter upbraiding, anxious inquiry, and frightened entreaty. The responsibility for the situation lay with him, and he must prevent matters from becoming worse. Could Tobermory impart his dangerous gift to other cats? was the first question he had to answer. It was possible, he replied, that he might have initiated his intimate friend the stable puss into his new accomplishment, but it was unlikely that his teaching could have taken a wider range as yet.

'Then,' said Mrs Cornett, 'Tobermory may be a valuable cat and a great pet; but I'm sure you'll agree, Adelaide, that both he and the stable cat must be done away with without delay.'

'You don't suppose I've enjoyed the last quarter of an hour, do you?' said Lady Blemley bitterly. 'My husband and I are very fond of Tobermory—at least, we were before this horrible accomplishment was infused into him; but now, of course, the only thing is to have him destroyed as soon as possible.'

'We can put some strychnine in the scraps he always gets at dinner time,' said Sir Wilfrid, 'and I will go and drown the stable cat myself. The coachman will be very sore at losing his pet, but I'll say a very catching form of mange has broken out in both cats and we're afraid of it spreading to the kennels.'

'But my great discovery!' expostulated Mr Appin; 'after all my years of research and experiment—'

'You can go and experiment on the short-horns at the farm, who are under proper control,' said Mrs Cornett, 'or the elephants at the Zoological Gardens. They're said to be highly intelligent, and they have this recommendation, that they don't come creeping about our bedrooms and under chairs, and so forth.'

An archangel ecstatically proclaiming the Millennium, and then finding that it clashed unpardonably with Henley and would have to be indefinitely postponed, could hardly have felt more crest-fallen than Cornelius Appin at the reception of his wonderful achievement. Public opinion, however, was against him—in fact, had the general voice been consulted on the subject it is probable that a strong minority vote would have been in favour of including him in the strychnine diet.

Defective train arrangements and a nervous desire to see matters brought to a finish prevented an immediate dispersal of the party, but dinner that evening was not a social success. Sir Wilfrid had had rather a trying time with the stable cat and subsequently with the coachman. Agnes Resker ostentatiously limited her repast to a morsel of dry toast, which she bit as though it were a personal enemy; while Mavis Pellington maintained a vindictive silence throughout the meal. Lady Blemley kept up a flow of what she hoped was conversation, but her attention was fixed on the door-way. A plateful of carefully dosed fish scraps was in readiness on the sideboard, but sweets and savoury and dessert went their way, and no Tobermory appeared either in the dining room or kitchen.

The sepulchral dinner was cheerful compared with the sub-sequent vigil in the smoking room. Eating and drinking had at least supplied a distraction and cloak to the prevailing embarrassment. Bridge was out of the question in the general tension of nerves and tempers, and after Odo Finsberry had given a lugubrious rendering of 'Mélisande in the Wood' to a frigid audience, music was tacitly avoided. At eleven the servants went to bed, announcing that the small window in the pantry had been left open as usual for Tobermory's private use. The guests read steadily through the current batch of magazines, and fell back gradually on the 'Badminton Library' and bound volumes of *Punch*. Lady Blemley made periodic visits to the pantry, returning each time with an expression of listless depression which forestalled questioning.

At two o'clock Clovis broke the dominating silence.

'He won't turn up tonight. He's probably in the local newspaper office at the present moment, dictating the first instalment of his reminiscences. Lady What's-her-name's book won't be in it. It will be the event of the day.'

Having made this contribution to the general cheerfulness, Clovis went to bed. At long intervals the various members of the house-party followed his example.

The servants taking round the early tea made a uniform announcement in reply to a uniform question. Tobermory had not returned.

Breakfast was, if anything, a more unpleasant function than dinner had been, but before its conclusion the situation was relieved. Tobermory's corpse was brought in from the shrubbery, where a gardener had just discovered it. From the bites on his throat and the yellow fur which coated his claws it was evident that he had fallen in unequal combat with the big Tom from the Rectory.

By midday most of the guests had quitted the Towers, and after lunch Lady Blemley had sufficiently recovered her spirits to write an extremely nasty letter to the Rectory about the loss of her valuable pet.

Tobermory had been Appin's one successful pupil, and he was destined to have no successor. A few weeks later an elephant in the Dresden Zoological Garden, which had shown no previous signs of irritability, broke loose and killed an Englishman who had apparently been teasing it. The victim's name was variously reported in the papers as Oppin and Eppelin, but his front name was faithfully rendered Cornelius.

'If he was trying German irregular verbs on the poor beast,' said Clovis, 'he deserved all he got.'

The Black Cat

For the most wild, yet most homely narrative which I am about to pen, I neither expect nor solicit belief. Mad indeed would I be to expect it, in a case where my very senses reject their own evidence. Yet, mad am I not—and very surely do I not dream. But tomorrow I die, and today I would unburden my soul. My immediate purpose is to place before the world, plainly, succinctly, and without comment, a series of mere household events. In their consequences, these events have terrified—have tortured—have destroyed me. Yet I will not attempt to expound them. To me, they have presented little but horror—to many they will seem less terrible than *baroques*. Hereafter, perhaps, some intellect may be found which will reduce my phantasm to the commonplace—some intellect more calm, more logical, and far less excitable than my own, which will perceive, in the circumstances I detail with awe, nothing more than an ordinary succession of very natural causes and effects.

From my infancy I was noted for the docility and humanity of my disposition. My tenderness of heart was even so conspicuous as to make me the jest of my companions. I was especially fond of animals, and was indulged by my parents with a great variety of pets. With these I spent most of my time, and never was so happy as when feeding and caressing them. This peculiarity of character grew with my growth, and, in my manhood, I derived from it one of my principal sources of pleasure. To those who have cherished an affection for a faithful and sagacious dog, I need hardly be at the trouble of explaining the nature or the intensity of the gratification thus derivable. There is something in the unselfish and self-sacrificing love of a brute, which goes directly to the heart of him who has had frequent occasion to test the paltry friendship and gossamer fidelity of mere *Man*.

I married early, and was happy to find in my wife a disposition not uncongenial with my own. Observing my partiality for domestic pets, she lost no opportunity of procuring those of the most agreeable kind. We had birds, goldfish, a fine dog, rabbits, a small monkey, and *a cat*.

This latter was a remarkably large and beautiful animal, entirely black, and sagacious to an astonishing degree. In speaking of his intelligence, my wife, who at heart was not a little tinctured with superstition, made frequent allusion to the ancient popular notion, which regarded all black cats as witches in disguise. Not that she was ever *serious* upon this point—and I mention the matter at all for no better reason than that it happens, just now, to be remembered.

Pluto—this was the cat's name—was my favourite pet and playmate. I alone fed him, and he attended me wherever I went about the house. It was even with difficulty that I could prevent him from following me through the streets.

Our friendship lasted, in this manner, for several years, during which my general temperament and character—through the instrumentality of the fiend Intemperance—had (I blush to confess it) experienced a radical alteration for the worse. I grew, day by day, more moody, more irritable, more regardless of the feelings of others. I suffered myself to use intemperate language to my wife. At length, I even offered her personal violence. My pets, of course, were made to feel the change in my disposition. I not only neglected, but ill-used them. For Pluto, however, I still retained sufficient regard to restrain me from maltreating him, as I made no scruple of maltreating the rabbits, the monkey, or even the dog, when by accident, or through affection, they came in my way. But my disease grew upon me—for what disease is like alcohol?—and at length even Pluto, who was now becoming old, and consequently somewhat peevish—even Pluto began to experience the effects of my ill temper.

One night, returning home, much intoxicated, from one of my haunts about town, I fancied that the cat avoided my presence. I seized him; when, in his fright at my violence he inflicted a slight wound upon my hand with his teeth. The fury of a demon instantly possessed me. I knew myself no longer. My original soul seemed, at once, to take its flight from my body; and a more than fiendish malevolence, gin-nurtured, thrilled every fibre of my frame. I took from my waistcoat pocket a penknife, opened it, grasped the poor beast by the throat, and deliberately cut one of its eyes from the socket! I blush, I burn, I shudder, while I pen the damnable atrocity.

When reason returned with the morning—when I had slept off the fumes of the night's debauch—I experienced a sentiment half of horror, half of remorse, for the crime of which I had been guilty;

but it was, at best, a feeble and equivocal feeling, and the soul remained untouched. I again plunged into excess, and soon drowned in wine all memory of the deed.

In the meantime the cat slowly recovered. The socket of the lost eye presented, it is true, a frightful appearance, but he no longer appeared to suffer any pain. He went about the house as usual, but, as might be expected, fled in extreme terror at my approach. I had so much of my old heart left, as to be at first grieved by this evident dislike on the part of a creature which had once so loved me. But this feeling soon gave place to irritation. And then came, as if to my final and irrevocable overthrow, the spirit of PERVERSENESS. Of this spirit philosophy takes no account. Yet I am not more sure that my soul lives, than I am that perverseness is one of the primitive impulses of the human heart—one of the indivisible primary faculties, or sentiments, which give direction to the character of man. Who has not, a hundred times, found himself committing a vile or a silly action, for no other reason than because he knows he should *not*? Have we not a perpetual inclination, in the teeth of our best judgement, to violate that which is *Law*, merely because we understand it to be such? This spirit of perverseness, I say, came to my final overthrow. It was this unfathomable longing of the soul to *vex itself*—to offer violence to its own nature—to do wrong for the wrong's sake only—that urged me to continue and finally to consummate the injury I had inflicted upon the unoffending brute. One morning, in cool blood, I slipped a noose about its neck and hung it to the limb of a tree—hung it with the tears streaming from my eyes, and with the bitterest remorse at my heart—hung it *because* I knew that it had loved me, and *because* I felt it had given me no reason of offence—hung it *because* I knew that in so doing I was committing a sin—a deadly sin that would so jeopardize my immortal soul as to place it—if such a thing were possible—even beyond the reach of the infinite mercy of the Most Merciful and Most Terrible God.

On the night of the day on which this cruel deed was done, I was aroused from sleep by the cry of 'Fire!' The curtains of my bed were in flames. The whole house was blazing. It was with great difficulty that my wife, a servant, and myself, made our escape from the conflagration. The destruction was complete. My entire worldly wealth was swallowed up, and I resigned myself thenceforward to despair.

I am above the weakness of seeking to establish a sequence of cause and effect between the disaster and the atrocity. But I am

detailing a chain of facts, and wish not to leave even a possible
link imperfect. On the day succeeding the fire, I visited the ruins.
The walls, with one exception, had fallen in. This exception was
found in a compartment wall, not very thick, which stood about
the middle of the house, and against which had rested the head
of my bed. The plastering had here, in great measure, resisted the
action of the fire—a fact which I attributed to its having been
recently spread. About this wall a dense crowd were collected, and
many persons seemed to be examining a particular portion of it
with very minute and eager attention. The words 'strange!' 'singu-
lar!' and other similar expressions, excited my curiosity. I
approached and saw, as if graven in bas-relief upon the white surface, the figure of a gigantic *cat*. The impression was given with
an accuracy truly marvellous. There was a rope about the animal's
neck.

When I first beheld this apparition—for I could scarcely regard
it as less—my wonder and my terror were extreme. But at length
reflection came to my aid. The cat, I remembered, had been hung
in a garden adjacent to the house. Upon the alarm of fire, this
garden had been immediately filled by the crowd—by some one
of whom the animal must have been cut from the tree and thrown,
through an open window, into my chamber. This had probably
been done with the view of arousing me from sleep. The falling
of other walls had compressed the victim of my cruelty into the
substance of the freshly-spread plaster; the lime of which, with the
flames and the *ammonia* from the carcass, had then accomplished
the portraiture as I saw it.

Although I thus readily accounted to my reason, if not altogether
to my conscience, for the startling fact just detailed, it did not the
less fail to make a deep impression upon my fancy. For months
I could not rid myself of the phantasm of the cat; and, during this
period, there came back into my spirit a half-sentiment that
seemed, but was not, remorse. I went so far as to regret the loss
of the animal, and to look about me, among the vile haunts which
I now habitually frequented, for another pet of the same species,
and of somewhat similar appearance, with which to supply its
place.

One night as I sat, half stupefied, in a den of more than infamy,
my attention was suddenly drawn to some black object, reposing
upon the head of one of the immense hogsheads of gin, or of rum,
which constituted the chief furniture of the apartment. I had been
looking steadily at the top of this hogshead for some minutes, and

what now caused me surprise was the fact that I had not sooner perceived the object thereupon. I approached it, and touched it with my hand. It was a black cat—a very large one—fully as large as Pluto, and closely resembling him in every respect but one. Pluto had not a white hair upon any portion of his body; but this cat had a large, although indefinite, splotch of white, covering nearly the whole region of the breast.

Upon my touching him, he immediately arose, purred loudly, rubbed against my hand, and appeared delighted with my notice. This, then, was the very creature of which I was in search. I at once offered to purchase it of the landlord; but this person made no claim to it—knew nothing of it—had never seen it before.

I continued my caresses, and when I prepared to go home, the animal evinced a disposition to accompany me. I permitted it to do so; occasionally stooping and patting it as I proceeded. When it reached the house it domesticated itself at once, and became immediately a great favourite with my wife.

For my own part, I soon found a dislike to it arising within me. This was just the reverse of what I had anticipated; but—I know not how or why it was—its evident fondness for myself rather disgusted and annoyed me. By slow degrees, these feelings of disgust and annoyance rose into the bitterness of hatred. I avoided the creature; a certain sense of shame, and the remembrance of my former deed of cruelty, preventing me from physically abusing it, I did not, for some weeks, strike, or otherwise violently ill-use it; but gradually—very gradually—I came to look upon it with unutterable loathing, and to flee silently from its odious presence, as from the breath of a pestilence.

What added, no doubt, to my hatred of the beast, was the discovery, on the morning after I brought it home, that, like Pluto, it also had been deprived of one of its eyes. This circumstance, however, only endeared it to my wife, who, as I have already said, possessed, in a high degree, that humanity of feeling which had once been my distinguishing trait, and the source of many of my simplest and purest pleasures.

With my aversion to this cat, however, its partiality for myself seemed to increase. It followed my footsteps with a pertinacity which it would be difficult to make the reader comprehend. Whenever I sat, it would crouch beneath my chair, or spring upon my knees, covering me with its loathsome caresses. If I arose to walk, it would get between my feet, and thus nearly throw me down, or, fastening its long and sharp claws in my dress, clamber, in this manner, to my breast. At such times, although I longed to destroy it with a blow, I was yet withheld from so doing, partly by a memory of my former crime, but chiefly—let me confess it at once—by absolute *dread* of the beast.

This dread was not exactly a dread of physical evil—and yet I should be at a loss how otherwise to define it. I am almost ashamed to own—yes, even in this felon's cell, I am almost ashamed to own—that the terror and horror with which the animal inspired me, had been heightened by one of the merest chimeras it would be possible to conceive. My wife had called my attention, more than once, to the character of the mark of white hair, of which I have spoken, and which constituted the sole visible difference between the strange beast and the one I had destroyed. The reader will remember that this mark, although large, had been originally very indefinite; but, by slow degrees—degrees nearly imperceptible, and which for a long time my reason struggled to reject as fanciful—it had, at length, assumed a rigorous distinctness of outline. It was now the representation of an object that I shudder to name—and for this, above all, I loathed, and dreaded, and would have rid myself of the monster *had I dared*—it was now, I say, the image of a hideous—of a ghastly thing—of the GALLOWS!—oh, mournful and terrible engine of horror and of crime—of agony and of death!

And now was I indeed wretched beyond the wretchedness of mere humanity. And *a brute beast*—whose fellow I had contemptuously destroyed—*a brute beast* to work out for *me*—for me, a man, fashioned in the image of the High God—so much of insufferable woe! Alas! neither by day nor by night knew I the blessing of rest any more! During the former the creature left me no moment alone; and, in the latter, I started, hourly, from dreams of unutterable fear, to find the hot breath of *the thing* upon my face, and its vast weight—an incarnate nightmare that I had no power to shake off—incumbent eternally upon my *heart!*

Beneath the pressure of torments such as these, the feeble remnant of the good within me succumbed. Evil thoughts became my sole intimates—the darkest and most evil of thoughts. The moodiness of my usual temper increased to hatred of all things and of all mankind; while, from the sudden, frequent, and ungovernable outbursts of a fury to which I now blindly abandoned myself, my uncomplaining wife, alas! was the most usual and the most patient of sufferers.

One day she accompanied me, upon some household errand,

into the cellar of the old building which our poverty compelled us to inhabit. The cat followed me down the steep stairs, and, nearly throwing me headlong, exasperated me to madness. Uplifting an axe, and forgetting, in my wrath, the childish dread which had hitherto stayed my hand, I aimed a blow at the animal which, of course, would have proved instantly fatal had it descended as I wished. But this blow was arrested by the hand of my wife. Goaded, by the interference, into a rage more than demoniacal, I withdrew my arm from her grasp, and buried the axe in her brain. She fell dead upon the spot, without a groan.

This hideous murder accomplished, I set myself forthwith, and with entire deliberation, to the task of concealing the body. I knew that I could not remove it from the house, either by day or by night, without the risk of being observed by the neighbours. Many projects entered my mind. At one period I thought of cutting the corpse into minute fragments, and destroying them by fire. At another, I resolved to dig a grave for it in the floor of the cellar. Again I deliberated about casting it into the well in the yard—about packing it in a box, as if merchandise, with the usual arrangements, and so getting a porter to take it from the house. Finally I hit upon what I considered a far better expedient than either of these. I determined to wall it up in the cellar—as the monks of the Middle Ages are recorded to have walled up their victims.

For a purpose such as this the cellar was well adapted. Its walls were loosely constructed, and had lately been plastered throughout with a rough plaster, which the dampness of the atmosphere had prevented from hardening. Moreover, in one of the walls was a projection, caused by a false chimney, or fireplace, that had been filled up, and made to resemble the rest of the cellar. I made no doubt that I could readily displace the bricks at this point, insert the corpse, and wall the whole up as before, so that no eye could detect anything suspicious.

And in this calculation I was not deceived. By means of a crowbar I easily dislodged the bricks, and, having carefully deposited the body against the inner wall, I propped it in that position, while, with little trouble, I relaid the whole structure as it originally stood. Having procured mortar, sand, and hair, with every possible precaution, I prepared a plaster which could not be distinguished from the old, and with this I very carefully went over the new brickwork. When I had finished, I felt satisfied that all was right. The wall did not present the slightest appearance of having been disturbed.

The rubbish on the floor was picked up with the minutest care. I looked around triumphantly, and said to myself, 'Here at least, then, my labour has not been in vain.'

My next step was to look for the beast which had been the cause of so much wretchedness; for I had, at length, firmly resolved to put it to death. Had I been able to meet with it, at the moment, there could have been no doubt of its fate; but it appeared that the crafty animal had been alarmed at the violence of my previous anger, and forbore to present itself in my present mood. It is impossible to describe, or to imagine, the deep, the blissful sense of relief which the absence of the detested creature occasioned in my bosom. It did not make its appearance during the night—and thus for one night at least, since its introduction into the house, I soundly and tranquilly slept; aye, *slept* even with the burden of murder upon my soul!

The second and the third day passed, and still my tormentor came not. Once again I breathed as a free man. The monster, in terror, had fled the premises for ever! I should behold it no more! My happiness was supreme! The guilt of my dark deed disturbed me but little. Some few inquiries had been made, but these had been readily answered. Even a search had been instituted—but of course nothing was to be discovered. I looked upon my future felicity as secured.

Upon the fourth day of the assassination, a party of the police came, very unexpectedly, into the house, and again to make rigorous investigation of the premises. Secure, however, in the inscrutability of my place of concealment, I felt no embarrassment whatever. The officers bade me accompany them in their search. They left no nook or corner unexplored. At length, for the third or fourth time, they descended into the cellar. I quivered not in a muscle. My heart beat calmly as that of one who slumbers in innocence. I walked the cellar from end to end. I folded my arms upon my bosom, and roamed easily to and fro. The police were thoroughly satisfied, and prepared to depart. The gleee at my heart was too strong to be restrained. I burned to say if but one word, by way of triumph, and to render doubly sure their assurance of my guiltlessness.

'Gentlemen,' I said at last, as the party ascended the steps, 'I delight to have allayed your suspicions. I wish you all health, and a little more courtesy. By-the-bye, gentlemen, this—this is a very well-constructed house.' (In the rabid desire to say something easily, I scarcely knew what I uttered at all.) 'I may say an *excellently* well-constructed house. These walls—are you going, gentle-men?—these walls are solidly put together'; and here, through the mere frenzy of bravado, I rapped heavily, with a cane which I held in my hand, upon that very portion of the brickwork behind which stood the corpse of the wife of my bosom.

But may God shield and deliver me from the fangs of the Arch-Fiend! No sooner had the reverberation of my blows sunk into silence, than I was answered by a voice from within the tomb!—by a cry, at first muffled and broken, like the sobbing of a child, and then quickly swelling into one long, loud, and continuous scream, utterly anomalous and inhuman—a howl—a wailing shriek, half of horror and half of triumph, such as might have arisen only out of hell, conjointly from the throats of the damned in their agony and of the demons that exult in the damnation.

Of my own thoughts it is folly to speak. Swooning, I staggered to the opposite wall. For one instant the party upon the stairs remained motionless, through extremity of terror and of awe. In the next, a dozen stout arms were toiling at the wall. It fell bodily. The corpse, already greatly decayed and clotted with gore, stood erect before the eyes of the spectators. Upon its head, with red extended mouth and solitary eye of fire, sat the hideous beast whose craft had seduced me into murder, and whose informing voice had consigned me to the hangman. I had walled the monster up within the tomb!

The Rain Horse

As the young man came over the hill the first thin blowing of rain met him. He turned his coat-collar up and stood on top of the shelving rabbit-riddled hedgebank, looking down into the valley.

He had come too far. What had set out as a walk along pleasantly remembered tarmac lanes had turned dreamily by gate and path and hedge-gap into a cross-ploughland trek, his shoes ruined, the dark mud of the lower fields inching up the trouser legs of his grey suit where they rubbed against each other. And now there was a raw, flapping wetness in the air that would be downpour again at any minute. He shivered, holding himself tense against the cold.

This was the view he had been thinking of. Vaguely, without really directing his walk, he had felt he would get the whole thing from this point. For twelve years, whenever he had recalled this scene, he had imagined it as it looked from here. Now the valley lay sunken in front of him, utterly deserted, shallow, bare fields, black and sodden as the bed of an ancient lake after the weeks of rain.

Nothing happened. Not that he had looked forward to any very transfiguring experience. But he had expected something, some pleasure, some meaningful sensation, he didn't quite know what.

So he waited, trying to nudge the right feelings alive with the details—the surprisingly familiar curve of the hedges, the stone gate-pillar and iron gatehook let into it that he had used as a target, the long bank of the rabbit warren on which he stood and which had been the first thing he ever noticed about the hill when twenty years ago, from the distance of the village, he had said to himself 'That looks like rabbits'.

Twelve years had changed him. This land no longer recognized him, and he looked back at it coldly, as at a finally visited home-country, known only through the stories of a grandfather; felt nothing but the dullness of feeling nothing. Boredom. Then, suddenly, impatience, with a whole exasperated swarm of little anxieties about his shoes and the spitting rain and his new suit and that sky and the two-mile trudge through the mud back to the road.

It would be quicker to go straight forward to the farm a mile away, in the valley and behind which the road looped. But the thought of meeting the farmer—to be embarrassingly remembered or shouted at as a trespasser—deterred him. He saw the rain pulling up out of the distance, dragging its grey broken columns, smudging the trees and the farms.

A wave of anger went over him: anger against himself for blundering into this mud-trap and anger against the land that made him feel so outcast, so old and stiff and stupid. He wanted nothing but to get away from it as quickly as possible. But as he turned, something moved in his eye-corner. All his senses startled alert. He stopped.

Over to his right a thin, black horse was running across the ploughland towards the hill, its head down, neck stretched out. It seemed to be running on its toes like a cat, like a dog up to no good.

From the high point on which he stood the hill dipped slightly and rose to another crested point fringed with the tops of trees, 300 yards to his right. As he watched it, the horse ran up that crest, showed against the sky—for a moment like a nightmarish leopard— and disappeared over the other side.

For several seconds he stared at the skyline, stunned by the unpleasantly strange impression the horse had made on him. Then the plastering beat of icy rain on his bare skull brought him to himself. The distance had vanished in a wall of grey. All around him the fields were jumping and streaming.

Holding his collar close and tucking his chin down into it he ran back over the hilltop towards the town side, the lee side, his feet sucking and splashing, at every stride plunging to the ankle.

This hill was shaped like a wave, a gently rounded back lifting out of the valley to a sharply crested, almost concave front hanging over the river meadows towards the town. Down this front, from the crest, hung two small woods separated by a fallow field. The near wood was nothing more than a quarry, circular, full of stones and bracken, with a few thorns and nondescript saplings, foxholes and rabbit holes. The other was rectangular, mainly a planting of scrub oak trees. Beyond the river smouldered the town like a great heap of blue cinders.

He ran along the top of the first wood and finding no shelter but the thin, leafless thorns of the hedge, dipped below the crest out of the wind and jogged along through thick grass to the wood of oaks. In blinding rain he lunged through the barricade of brambles at the wood's edge. The little crippled trees were small choice in the way of shelter, but at a sudden fierce thickening of the rain he took one at random and crouched down under the leaning trunk.

Still panting from his run, drawing his knees up tightly, he watched the bleak lines of rain, grey as hail, slanting through the boughs into the clumps of bracken and bramble. He felt hidden and safe. The sound of the rain as it rushed and lulled in the wood seemed to seal him in. Soon the chilly sheet lead of his suit became a tight, warm mould, and gradually he sank into a state of comfort that was all but trance, though the rain beat steadily on his exposed shoulders and trickled down the oak trunk on to his neck.

All around him the boughs angled down, glistening, black as iron. From their tips and elbows the drops hurried steadily, and the channels of the bark pulsed and gleamed. For a time he amused himself calculating the variation in the rainfall by the variations in a dribble of water from a trembling twig-end two feet in front of his nose. He studied the twig, bringing dwarfs and continents and animals out of its scurfy bark. Beyond the boughs the blue shoal of the town was rising and falling, and darkening and fading again, in the pale, swaying backdrop of rain.

He wanted this rain to go on for ever. Whenever it seemed to be drawing off he listened anxiously until it closed in again. As long as it lasted he was suspended from life and time. He didn't want to return to his sodden shoes and his possibly ruined suit and the walk back over that land of mud.

All at once he shivered. He hugged his knees to squeeze out the cold and found himself thinking of the horse. The hair on the nape of his neck prickled slightly. He remembered how it had run up to the crest and showed against the sky.

He tried to dismiss the thought. Horses wander about the countryside often enough. But the image of the horse as it had appeared against the sky stuck in his mind. It must have come over the crest just above the wood in which he was now sitting. To clear his mind, he twisted around and looked up the wood between the tree stems, to his left.

At the wood top, with the silvered grey light coming in behind it, the black horse was standing under the oaks, its head high and alert, its ears pricked, watching him.

A horse sheltering from the rain generally goes into a sort of stupor, tilts a hind hoof and hangs its head and lets its eyelids droop, and so it stays as long as the rain lasts. This horse was nothing like that. It was watching him intently, standing perfectly still, its soaked neck and flank shining in the hard light.

He turned back. His scalp went icy and he shivered. What was he to do? Ridiculous to try driving it away. And to leave the wood, with the rain still coming down full pelt was out of the question. Meanwhile the idea of being watched became more and more unsettling until at last he had to twist around again, to see if the horse had moved. It stood exactly as before.

This was absurd. He took control of himself and turned back deliberately, determined not to give the horse one more thought. If it wanted to share the wood with him, let it. If it wanted to stare at him, let it. He was nestling firmly into these resolutions when the ground shook and he heard the crash of a heavy body coming down the wood. Like lightning his legs bounded him upright and about face. The horse was almost on top of him, its head stretching forward, ears flattened and lips lifted back from the long yellow teeth. He got one snapshot glimpse of the red-veined eyeball as he flung himself backwards around the tree. Then he was away up the slope, whipped by oak twigs as he leapt the brambles and brushwood, twisting between the close trees till he tripped and sprawled. As he fell the warning flashed through his head that he must at all costs keep his suit out of the leaf-mould, but a more urgent instinct was already rolling him violently sideways. He spun around, sat up and looked back, ready to scramble off in a flash to one side. He was panting from the sudden excitement and effort. The horse had disappeared. The wood was empty except for the drumming, slant grey rain, dancing the bracken and glittering from the branches.

He got up, furious. Knocking the dirt and leaves from his suit as well as he could he looked around for a weapon. The horse was evidently mad, had an abscess on its brain or something of the sort. Or maybe it was just spiteful. Rain sometimes puts creatures into queer states. Whatever it was, he was going to get away from the wood as quickly as possible, rain or no rain.

Since the horse seemed to have gone on down the wood, his way to the farm over the hill was clear. As he went, he broke a yard length of wrist-thick dead branch from one of the oaks, but immediately threw it aside and wiped the slime of rotten wet bark from his hands with his soaked handkerchief. Already he was thinking it incredible that the horse could have meant to attack him. Most likely it was just going down the wood for better shelter and had made a feint at him in passing—as much out of curiosity or playfulness as anything. He recalled the way horses menace each other when they are galloping round in a paddock.

The wood rose to a steep bank topped by the hawthorn hedge that ran along the whole ridge of the hill. He was pulling himself up to a thin place in the hedge by the bare stem of one of the hawthorns when he ducked and shrank down again. The swelling gradient of fields lay in front of him, smoking in the slowly crossing rain. Out in the middle of the first field, tall as a statue, and a ghostly silver in the undercloud light, stood the horse, watching the wood.

He lowered his head slowly, slithered back down the bank and crouched. An awful feeling of helplessness came over him. He felt certain the horse had been looking straight at him. Waiting for him? Was it clairvoyant? Maybe a mad animal can be clairvoyant. At the same time he was ashamed to find himself acting so inanely, ducking and creeping about in this way just to keep out of sight of a horse. He tried to imagine how anybody in their senses would just walk off home. This cooled him a little, and he retreated farther down the wood. He would go back the way he had come, along under the hill crest, without any more nonsense.

The wood hummed and the rain was a cold weight, but he observed this rather than felt it. The water ran down inside his clothes and squelched in his shoes as he eased his way carefully over the bedded twigs and leaves. At every instant he expected to see the prick-eared black head looking down at him from the hedge above.

At the woodside he paused, close against a tree. The success of this last manœuvre was restoring his confidence, but he didn't want to venture out into the open field without making sure that the horse was just where he had left it. The perfect move would be to withdraw quietly and leave the horse standing out there in the rain. He crept up again among the trees to the crest and peered through the hedge.

The grey field and the whole slope were empty. He searched the distance. The horse was quite likely to have forgotten him altogether and wandered off. Then he raised himself and leaned out to see if it had come in close to the hedge. Before he was aware of anything the ground shook. He twisted around wildly to see how he had been caught. The black shape was above him, right across the light. Its whinnying snort and the spattering whack of its hooves seemed to be actually inside his head as he fell backwards down the bank, and leapt again like a madman, dodging among the oaks, imagining how the buffet would come and how he would be knocked headlong. Halfway down the wood the oaks gave way to bracken and old roots and stony rabbit diggings. He was well out into the middle of this before he realized that he was running alone.

Gasping for breath now and cursing mechanically, without a thought for his suit he sat down on the ground to rest his shaking legs, letting the rain plaster the hair down over his forehead and watching the dense flashing lines disappear abruptly into the soil all around him as if he were watching through thick plate glass. He took deep breaths in the effort to steady his heart and regain control of himself. His right trouser turnup was ripped at the seam and his suit jacket was splashed with the yellow mud of the top field.

Obviously the horse had been farther along the hedge above the steep field, waiting for him to come out at the woodside just as he had intended. He must have peeped through the hedge—peeping the wrong way—within yards of it.

However, this last attack had cleared up one thing. He need no longer act like a fool out of mere uncertainty as to whether the horse was simply being playful or not. It was definitely after him. He picked two stones about the size of goose eggs and set off towards the bottom of the wood, striding carelessly.

A loop of the river bordered all this farmland. If he crossed the little level meadow at the bottom of the wood, he could follow the three-mile circuit, back to the road. There were deep hollows in the river-bank, shoaled with pebbles, as he remembered, perfect places to defend himself from if the horse followed him out there.

The hawthorns that choked the bottom of the wood—some of them good-sized trees—knitted into an almost impassable barrier. He had found a place where the growth thinned slightly and had begun to lift aside the long spiny stems, pushing himself forward, when he stopped. Through the bluish veil of bare twigs he saw the familiar shape out in the field below the wood.

But it seemed not to have noticed him yet. It was looking out across the field towards the river. Quietly, he released himself from the thorns and climbed back across the clearing towards the one side of the wood he had not yet tried. If the horse would only stay down there he could follow his first and easiest plan, up the wood and over the hilltop to the farm.

Now he noticed that the sky had grown much darker. The rain was heavier every second, pressing down as if the earth had to be flooded before nightfall. The oaks ahead blurred and the ground drummed. He began to run. And as he ran he heard a deeper sound running with him. He whirled around. The horse was in the middle of the clearing. It might have been running to get out of the terrific rain except that it was coming straight for him, scattering clay and stones, with an immensely supple and powerful motion. He let out a tearing roar and threw the stone in his right hand. The result was instantaneous. Whether at the roar or the stone the horse reared as if against a wall and shied to the left. As it dropped back on to its forefeet he flung his second stone, at ten yards' range, and saw a bright mud blotch suddenly appear on the glistening black flank. The horse surged down the wood, splashing the earth like water, tossing its long tail as it plunged out of sight among the hawthorns.

He looked around for stones. The encounter had set the blood beating in his head and given him a savage energy. He could have killed the horse at that moment. That this brute should pick him and play with him in this malevolent fashion was more than he could bear. Whoever owned it, he thought, deserved to have its neck broken for letting the dangerous thing loose.

He came out at the woodside, in open battle now, still searching for the right stones. There were plenty here, piled and scattered where they had been ploughed out of the field. He selected two, then straightened and saw the horse twenty yards off in the middle of the steep field, watching him calmly. They looked at each other.

'Out of it!' he shouted, brandishing his arm. 'Out of it! Go on!' The horse twitched its pricked ears. With all his force he threw. The stone soared and landed beyond with a soft thud. He re-armed and threw again. For several minutes he kept up his bombardment without a single hit, working himself up into a despair and throwing more and more wildly, till his arm began to ache with the unaccustomed exercise. Throughout the performance the horse watched him fixedly. Finally he had to stop and ease his shoulder muscles. As if the horse had been waiting for just this, it dipped its head twice and came at him.

He snatched up two stones and roaring with all his strength flung the one in his right hand. He was astonished at the crack of the impact. It was as if he had struck a tile—and the horse actually stumbled. With another roar he jumped forward and hurled his other stone. His aim seemed to be under superior guidance. The stone struck and rebounded straight up into the air, spinning fiercely, as the horse swirled away and went careering down towards the far bottom corner of the field, at first with great, swinging leaps, then at a canter, leaving deep churned holes in the soil.

It turned up the far side of the field, climbing till it was level with him. He felt a little surprise of pity to see it shaking its head, and once it paused to lower its head and paw over its ear with its forehoof as a cat does.

'You stay there!' he shouted. 'Keep your distance and you'll not get hurt.'

And indeed the horse did stop at that moment, almost obediently. It watched him as he climbed to the crest.

The rain swept into his face and he realized that he was freezing, as if his very flesh were sodden. The farm seemed miles away over the dreary fields. Without another glance at the horse—he felt too exhausted to care now what it did—he loaded the crook of his left arm with stones and plunged out on to the waste of mud.

He was halfway to the first hedge before the horse appeared, silhouetted against the sky at the corner of the wood, head high and attentive, watching his laborious retreat over the three fields.

The ankle-deep clay dragged at him. Every stride was a separate, deliberate effort, forcing him up and out of the sucking earth, burdened as he was by his sogged clothes and load of stones and limbs that seemed themselves to be turning to mud. He fought to keep his breathing even, two strides in, two strides out, the air ripping his lungs. In the middle of the last field he stopped and looked around. The horse, tiny on the skyline, had not moved.

At the corner of the field he unlocked his clasped arms and dumped the stones by the gatepost, then leaned on the gate. The farm was in front of him. He became conscious of the rain again and suddenly longed to stretch out full-length under it, to take the cooling, healing drops all over his body and forget himself in the last wretchedness of the mud. Making an effort he heaved his weight over the gate-top. He leaned again, looking up at the hill.

Rain was dissolving land and sky together like a wet watercolour as the afternoon darkened. He concentrated, raising his head, searching the skyline from end to end. The horse had vanished. The hill looked lifeless and desolate, an island lifting out of the sea, awash with every tide.

Under the long shed where the tractors, plough, binders and the rest were drawn up, waiting for their seasons, he sat on a sack thrown over a petrol drum, trembling, his lungs heaving. The mingled smell of paraffin, creosote, fertilizer, dust—all was exactly as he had left it twelve years ago. The ragged swallows' nests were still there tucked in the angles of the rafters. He remembered three dead foxes hanging in a row from one of the beams, their teeth bloody.

The ordeal with the horse had already sunk from reality. It hung under the surface of his mind, an obscure confusion of fright and shame, as after a narrowly escaped street accident. There was a solid pain in his chest, like a spike of bone stabbing, that made him wonder if he had strained his heart on that last stupid burdened run. Piece by piece he began to take off his clothes, wringing the grey water out of them, but soon he stopped that and just sat staring at the ground, as if some important part had been cut out of his brain.

David Stephen

The Red Stranger

It was cubbing time in the big badger cairn on the Ben of Mists, though the snow still lay deep in the high corries and swept in clouds of white powder before the savage, scourging winds on the tops. Up there, among the rocks, the naked aspen roots were still clawed with icicles, and every mountain cascade was silent, its falling water turned to columns and pillars of ice that glowed with rainbow fire in the sun.

Countless generations of badger cubs had been born in the wild, rocky cairn, the age or depth of which no man knew, for a badger set can be old as a town is old, and as steeped in history.

The den on the Ben of Mists was old when the Great Montrose swept down the Garry to Athole.... Dundee had rested where the badgers foraged before his falcon swoop to death and victory at Killiecrankie.... And, later still, but still more than two centuries ago, the sunning Brocks had hearkened to the faint, far skirl of the Highland War Pipes when the clansmen proudly marched to death and exile under the banner of Royal Tearlach....

Bodach, the old boar badger, king of the cairn, was lying one morning in a rocky hollow, sucking a forepaw in sleep, sunning himself out of reach of the wind. Night-hunter though he was, and born of a line that had prowled by night for a thousand years, he still liked the feel of the sun, and in that quiet stronghold on the Ben of Mists he could take the risk of such a luxury.

Below, far inside the cairn, his mate lay curled with her three small, helpless cubs, on a fresh, sweet bed of grass and withered bracken which she had laboriously carried into the den. The galleries of the set were long and tortuous, and in their dark shelter lay two other female badgers nursing cubs. In all, the den held three nursing females; three boars which were their mates; and two young males of the previous year. And Bodach was the chief by virtue of age and prowess.

The wind eddied into Bodach's hollow in spent breaths, ruffling the grey hair of his back and bringing messages to his wet nose. And, quite suddenly, he awoke, grunting and releasing his paw, for his nose had just owned a scent that he didn't like—a scent that spelt trouble.

Over the rocks of the cairn came a big hill vixen—red of leg and long of jaw, with her tongue out and her brush down, hirpling along on three legs. Bodach smelt her strong musky odour; he could also smell her blood. But it is doubtful if he realized that her left forepaw was a bloody stump which throbbed more agonizingly than an aching tooth. The vixen had just chewed herself from a gin set by the keeper, and had left three toes and four claws behind.

And now she was seeking refuge in the cairn of the badgers!

Bodach didn't like her; and I'm sure he didn't want her. But when she crawled into one of the entrance holes of the set, he made no move to stop her.

Perhaps he realized she was wounded. He may even have realized that she would be sought for by the men who had set the gin. He had had foxes in the set before, and didn't like their dirty habits—their way of cluttering up the tunnels with bits and pieces of prey. In the past he had tolerated such lodgers for a time, then driven them out with threatening jaws. Yet, on this occasion, he appeared to be quite indifferent to the presence of a wounded vixen who was wanted by Man!

Bodach sat for some minutes, swaying from side to side like a bear; then he shambled underground to his mate, who had already got news of the fox with her nose and knew the vixen was in the cairn.

The red stranger crawled slowly down a side tunnel, one which was not being used by the badgers, but which was really a grave-yard for the clan. For many dead badgers were walled up in the tunnel, carefully buried from sight in side pockets dug by the feet of Bodach and his ancestors.

At last the vixen found a hollow beneath an outcrop of rock and there she lay down to lick her foot.

No badger came to her during all that day, but she heard them leaving after dusk on their hunting trips. Throughout the night she did not stir, being too preoccupied with her aching paw. By the next afternoon she was wild with hunger, for she, too, was about to become a mother. But how could she hope to hunt in her condition?

Such thoughts may not have occurred to her, but she certainly made no effort to strike out on her own when she left the den at nightfall. Instead she took up the trail of old Bodach, and followed it.

She was going to play jackal to the badger!

That night, Bodach went down a thousand feet into the glen, where the deer were feeding on the sward by the river. He knew it was useless to hunt upwards, for wind and snow had driven every-thing down, and whether he wanted vegetable or flesh food he was forced to hunt the valleys. And limping slowly in his wake, keeping in touch with her nose, went the vixen.

The lower slopes were cleared forest, and big herds of deer were feeding among millions of tree-stumps and along avenues of weathered, layered branches. Mountain hares were feeding there, too, but they were too fleet for Bodach and he ignored them. The vixen's jaws dripped water but she knew she had no hope of stalking hares for many nights to come.

Bodach gobbled beetles and slugs that he found in the grass. He found the remains of a grouse that had been killed by a falcon and crouched down to eat it, warning off the vixen with grunts and thunderous growls. She made no move to interfere. She was con-tent to wait.

And, in due course, her patience was rewarded. Bodach found the entrance to a rabbit nest, or 'stop', under a clutter of old branches. He sniffed at the earth-stopped entrance, scraped away a little soil, and satisfied himself there were rabbits inside. But he didn't start to dig at the mouth of the burrow.

Instead, he crashed through the branches, and started to heave them aside with his powerful forepaws. When he had cleared a space in which he could manoeuvre, he started to dig straight down, and the sand and pebbles and grass roots flew from under his strong, bear claws. He was digging a shaft right down on to the rabbit's nest!

In a few moments he had the nest uncovered. A few seconds more, and he was clawing the young rabbits from their bed of grass and wool. The vixen sat impassively while he dug, but when he had scattered five young rabbits on the branches she moved in to mooch.

At first he grunted at her, for all the world like a rooting pig. But once he was settled, chewing on one rabbit while holding on to two others with his claws, he let her sneak in and filch the remaining two. Snarling, she drew back, and she had swallowed both rabbits before Bodach started on his second. The food was a godsend to her, for she could not have dug the rabbits out by herself that night. But, instead of appreciating Bodach's generosity, she tried to snatch a third rabbit from under his nose.

Bodach, however, had had enough of her, and when he rose, showing his teeth, she knew she had gone as far as she dared. With a parting snarl at her benefactor she turned away and limped slowly back to the cairn, leaving Bodach to his own devices for the rest of the night.

And so it was, night after night, for the next week; the vixen was Bodach's shadow. Not once did she follow the other boar badgers, or the nursing sows. It was always Bodach; and not once did the old badger try to drive her away.

Of course, when he found food, he always warned her off, and if there was not enough for two she had to do without.

In this way she eked out a living; but it didn't make her fat, for Bodach spent as much time in the low woods digging for bluebell bulbs as he did ranging the glen for rabbit nests or carrion. And, when he was on vegetable food like that, the vixen had to go to bed with an empty belly.

One night, when Bodach took a new route, he found the remains of a red deer hind, on which ravens and crows had been feasting for days. Badger and fox ate their fill of old venison that night and afterwards the vixen drank greedily. It was the stoutest meal she had eaten for a week. But when she went back the following night, without the badger, she found that the last remains had been devoured by the carrion birds during the day.

Disgruntled, her thoughts turned at once to the badger, so she limped away to seek him in the glen. It was close on daybreak before she found him, and he was carrying in his jaws the fore end of a mountain hare—the remains of an eagle's prey! Bodach knew the daylight was not far off so he was carrying his prize to a spot nearer home where he could devour it at leisure. He had an objection to being caught far from home in daylight.

The vixen couldn't get near him on the way home. Time after time he stopped to swear at her, and she was too wise to force her attentions on him. In a hollow, about a hundred yards below the cairn, Bodach finally stopped and lay down to eat his meal, for it was against all his cleanly principles to take food right into his den.

Replete at last, he left the remains of his prey and hurried home as fast as his short legs would carry him. And, of course, the vixen snatched up the leavings. And being a fox, she had none of the badger's scruples, so she carried her prey to the cairn and vanished inside with it in her jaws.

Now, if she had been well enough to keep bringing prey home

like that, it is probable Bodach would have thrown her out for her dirty housekeeping. However, before she could commit a second offence, badgers and fox had other things to worry about.

One morning, the dwellers in the cairn heard the ominous tread of nailed boots on the rocks above, then the voices of men, followed by the sharp yelping of terriers. The sow badgers cuddled closer to their cubs; four boars crouched wondering; the vixen drew back into the narrowest neck of her tunnel; and Bodach mounted guard at the main entrance to the nurseries. Bodach was old; he knew what was coming; and he knew how to deal with it.

Above ground were two keepers, the shepherd, and two terriers. The keepers had no quarrel with the badgers, and were doubtful about letting the terriers into the set to try to oust the fox. They knew what a baited badger could do.

'She had to pick here, of course!' grumbled Macdonald, the head keeper, rubbing his chin.

'Weel, there it is!' commented the shepherd. 'It was pure chance I was spying the hill, and there she was on the rocks, sore foot and all. What d'you think, Mac?'

'She'll no' trap, that's certain!' interjected Fraser, the under-keeper. 'That foot's a' the lesson she needs.'

Macdonald was perturbed.

'If the brocks stay clear the terriers micht bolt her. But they'll have cubs, and I canna see them standing by idle if the dogs take the wrong turning. Still, I suppose we'll have to try....'

The first dog was slipped—Nip, a small, lean Border terrier with a much-scarred mask. Fearlessly she darted into the den, and the men stood back with shotguns at the ready.

Down below there was fear among the badgers, but no panic. The sows started digging frantically, to put earth and distance behind them; the boars dug, all except Bodach, who stood four-square on the threshold of the nurseries; the red vixen waited, hoping....

But she was unlucky. The terrier, knowing her business, found the tunnel leading to the fox, and by-passed the waiting badger. Soon her frenzied barking signalled to the waiting men that she had found her fox.

The big vixen drew back hard against the tunnel wall, and presented her sharp muzzle to the foe. The terrier rushed in, chopping and girning, but the fox met her teeth and gave as good as she got. Blood appeared on her mask, but not all of it her own.

Realizing she couldn't get behind the fox, Nip crouched low, yapping, to stampede her opponent into some kind of forward move. But the vixen was cunning; she had been baited before. She was content to leave the offensive to the dog.

The terrier's frenzied yapping told the men much. They knew the vixen was cornered but refusing to bolt.

'We'll leave her a wee,' said Mac, who realized the dog had only the fox to deal with.

For several minutes dog and fox faced each other—the little bitch barking, the vixen mute. Then the terrier worked herself into such a pitch of rage that she darted to the clinch.

The fox's teeth opened Nip's skin above the eye; they tore her ear; they clashed against her tusks. But the terrier was in and under, blind to the bites, and in a moment was gurrying through the vixen's ruff for her throat.

Her teeth found skin, and gripped, and locked. The vixen chop-chopped at her attacker's flank, scoring with her tusk; but she couldn't reach round far enough for a wounding bite. So she moved forward, taking the dog with her, and presently they were a locked, squirming mass of fur—growling, snarling, shaking.

The terrier hung on grimly, growling through locked teeth. But presently the vixen gained the wider part of the tunnel, where she could move faster. In her blind rush for the open, she rubbed against a projecting rock. The rock got the terrier in the ribs and she lost her grip. And the vixen was clear.

But...

What was this blocking the way out? It was Bodach, filling the tunnel with his bulk, standing there with head lowered, waiting....

For what? For the fox? No, not for the fox, for he let the vixen squeeze past without demur. He was waiting for the dog!

Game though she was, the little terrier was no match for the big boar badger of the Ben of Mists, especially in her weakened state. And she knew it. But the knowledge didn't deter her, and she shaped up to Bodach, bristling, with teeth bared to the gums, a brave fighter meeting another brave fighter with all the advantage of size and ground on the badger's side.

At the first clash, the terrier's jaws gathered nothing but grey hair from the badger's shoulder. But Bodach's jaws tore skin and flesh from the terrier's face, and her howling was heard by the men at the den mouth above.

At first the men couldn't understand what was happening. Then they caught a glimpse of the vixen at the mouth of the set, before

she turned into another tunnel. And they knew the terrier was face
to face with a badger.

'She's on to a badger,' said Mac. 'And maybe behind him, whatever. Send in Sheila, quick!'

The second dog needed no encouragement. She was in like a
flash, and down, rushing to the help of her kennel mate. And in
a moment she was behind the badger.

Now, a badger's hide is thick and tough, and the teeth of a terrier
do not make much impression on it. But a badger has one weak
spot, a spot he doesn't like touched at all—his scut. He is sensitive
about this little tail. Bodach was no exception. When he felt Sheila's
teeth at his tail he turned to face her.

She backed away, of course, and he charged at her, chopping
with his terrible teeth. But he now had two terriers to deal with,
and no sooner was he engaged with Sheila than he felt other teeth
at his scut. So he had to keep thrusting forward to find a spot where
he could get them both in front of him.

Bodach didn't panic. It wasn't his nature. He was a stoic, a
gentleman, and brave as they come. But his tail was worrying him.
He had to get it out of reach of the dogs.

The dogs, on the other hand, knew they had him at a disadvan-
tage, and they meant to keep him there. So while the dog at the
rear, the gallant little Nip, kept worrying at Bodach's back, Sheila
kept biting, and getting bitten, at his front.

But it couldn't last. The badger turned suddenly, realizing he
could rush Nip to the blind end of the tunnel and worry her there.
He swept her before him. It seemed she must die down there with
no one to come to her aid. But there was still Sheila.

As if realizing the badger's intention, she leaped at his rump,
and worried and bit till she really stung him to anger. For the first
time in his life he was really being worsted. So he turned yet again
to deal with the attacker at his back. But in that instant Nip rushed
at him, and whether by accident or design, squeezed past him to
join Sheila at the front.

The dogs were now assured of a line of retreat; the exit was
at their back. It was as well for them that this was so, for
Bodach now had them where he wanted them—in front of him.
With his rear secure, he kept inching towards them with his sharp
face well down, striking to right and left with the speed of a
snake, forcing them to yield ground or run the risk of a broken
jaw.

The terriers yapped and snarled, but kept edging slowly back, for they had no way of getting round Bodach's guard, and they knew the terrible punishing power of his teeth.

As they neared the mouth of the set, Bodach speeded up his offensive, carrying the fight right to the dogs. The first inkling the waiting men had of the truth was when the dogs came hurrying out backwards, closely followed by a badger reaching for their throats.

Macdonald instantly called off the dogs. They came bellying up to him reluctantly, with teeth bared and hackles raised. The keeper swore when he saw how they were cut up, then turned to where Bodach crouched, watching, with chin up and the light of battle in his small, bright eyes.

'Don't shoot him! he shouted to the under-keeper, who had lifted his gun. He turned back to the badger. 'Take that, you auld scunner!' he said, setting Bodach in motion with a well-placed toe on the rump. 'Now, off with you!'

Bodach blinked, and kept moving. He shambled quickly into the set, affronted at the indignity. He must have been the only badger who had ever had a man's toe in his seat!

'What now?' asked Fraser, the under-keeper. 'Traps?'

'Not here,' replied Macdonald. 'We'd only take the badgers. The fox'll shove them out first. You'll have to try baited traps in the peat hags. That vixen'll be looking for easy meat for a while yet.'

The traps were set that night—three of them—baited with grouse, placed on built-up hummocks in peat hags, on to which the fox would have to jump to reach the prize. But, as it happened, the jaws of the traps waited in vain for her feet.

That night a blizzard raged out of the north-east, turning the tops into a swirling white chaos and muffling the glens under a deep mantle of new snow. It blew itself out on the afternoon of the second day, and only then did badgers and fox emerge to view the world.

The tops were white, the cold intense, and the moon rising clear. Bodach struck off along the mountain-side, with only a vague idea of where he was going, and determined at worst to scrape through the snow for grass and blaeberries. And a little way behind, printing her own neat sign alongside the badger's bear-like tracks, limped the vixen....

Right into trouble....

They were on the lip of a small corrie, following a deer path already pounded by hoofs since the snowfall, when the pack-cry reached their ears. It came faintly at first, like the chipping of flints, menacing....

Bodach stopped, weaving his snout like a bear. The vixen halted, rigid, with ears up and nose questing. Soon, all too soon, the cry became louder . . . followed by musk smell . . . crimson eyes flickering on and off the moonshine . . . then the rippling movements of stoats gliding over the snow . . . eleven of them, some still white, some on the change to russet . . . but all wild with famine, all dangerous, a family united by hunger. . . .

They met Bodach because Bodach was in front. They swarmed round him, hissing, spitting, chattering, with teeth bared and black-tipped tails rigid. Bodach crouched, with hind feet drawn well in and head down, waiting. The big dog stoat who was the spearhead of the pack chattered loudly and the pack broke over Bodach in a wave.

The badger moved only his black-striped head—and his jaws. He kept his hind legs in because he had no wish to be hamstrung. Stoats bit at his head, his back, his rump—but his hide was impervious to their teeth. They hissed in his ear. Their musk nauseated him. But while they fumed he was chopping, and he broke the backs of three stoats in ninety seconds, while the remainder were gathering mouthfuls of grey, bristly hair.

With three stoats kicking and doing a death dance in the snow, Bodach was prepared to sit till the eight on his back came within reach of his jaws. But, presently, they became more selective in their attack. They found his ears—and his scut. They bit both. They stung him to white-hot fury. He rose to fight. And in a moment they were round his legs, under his guard, under his scut. . . .

He killed two more, and bit snow to get the horrible taste from his mouth. Then he started to spin round, reaching for them with his jaws.

At this moment the vixen intervened. She had been sitting on her tail twenty paces away, sizing up the situation. She could have retreated. She had time. But she didn't. Inexplicably, she went voluntarily into the fight.

Her jaws were lightning swift. She was agile. No slow-moving, stoical badger this. She chopped two more stoats, and in so doing diverted the attack to herself. As the four leaped at her she drew back to keep them in front of her, and waited for them with tusks bared and eyes closed to slits.

She was on the brink of the corrie when they struck her, where the snow was sculpted into eaves by the wind. She met them with snapping jaws, and wounded forepaw raised as a guard. As she snatched one in her jaws, three flashed in and had her by jowl and ruff. Then the snow-eave gave way....

For a moment it seemed to hang in the air above the corrie, then it fell clear and down, and the vixen, with her three stoats at her neck and one falling from her jaws, went with it, spinning through the air with brush flying. And, presently, there was a snow-muffled thud on the rocks fifty feet below.

The red stranger had paid her debt in full....

H. E. Bates

The White Pony

Alexander went down the farm-yard past the hay stacks and the bramble cart-shed and out into the field beyond the sycamore trees, looking for the white pony. The mist of the summer morning lay cottoned far across the valley, so that he moved in a world above clouds that seemed to float upward and envelop him as he went down the slope. Here and there he came across places in the grass where the pony had lain during the night, buttercups and moon-daisies pressed flat as in a prayer-book by the fat flanks, and he could see where hoofs had broken the ground by stamping and had exploded the ginger ant-hills. But there was no white pony. The mist was creeping rapidly up the field and soon he could see nothing except grass and the floating foam of white and golden flowers flowing as on a smooth tide out of the mist, and could hear nothing except the blunted voices of birds in the deep mist-silence of the fields.

The pony was a week old. Somewhere, for someone else, he had had another life, but for Alexander it had no meaning. All of his life that mattered had begun from the minute, a week past, when Uncle Bishop had bought him to replace the rough chestnut, and a new life had begun for Alexander. To the boy the white pony was now a miracle. 'See how straight he stands,' he had heard a man say. 'Breedin' there. Mighta bin a race-horse.' They called him Snowy, and he began to call the name as he went down the field, singing it, low and high, inverting the sound of the cuckoos coming from the spinneys. But there was still no pony and he went down to the farthest fences without seeing him. The pony had been there, kicking white scars into the ashpales sometime not long before, leaving fresh mushrooms of steaming dung in the grass. The boy stood swinging the halter like a lasso, wishing it could be a lasso and he himself a wild boy alone in a wild world.

After a minute he moved away, calling again, wondering a little, and at that instant the mist swung upwards. It seemed to lift with the suddenness of a released balloon, leaving the field suffused with warm apricot light, the daisies china-white in the sun, and in the centre of it the white pony standing dead still, feet together, head splendid aloof and erect, a statue of chalk.

Seeing him, Alexander ran across the field, taking two haunches of bread out of his pocket as he went. The pony waited, not moving. 'Snowy,' the boy said, 'Snowy.' He held the bread out in one hand flat, touching the pony's nose with the other, and the pony lowered his head and took the bread, the teeth warm and slimy on the palm of the boy's hand. After the bread had gone, Alexander fixed the halter. 'Snowy,' he kept saying, 'Good boy, Snowy,' deeply glad of the moment of being alone there with the horse, smelling the strong warm horse smell, feeling the sun already warm on his own neck and on the body of the horse as he led him away.

Back at the fence he drew the horse closely parallel to the rails and then climbed up and got on. He sat well up, knees bent. The flanks of the pony under his bare knees seemed smoother and more friendly than anything on earth and as he moved forward the boy felt that he and the pony were part of each other, indivisible in a new affection. He moved gently and as the boy called him again 'Snowy, giddup, Snowy,' the ears flickered and were still in a second of response and knowledge. And suddenly, from the new height of the pony's back, the boy felt extraordinarily excited and solitary, completely alone in the side of the valley, with the sun breaking the mist and the fields lining up into distant battalions of colour and the farms waking beyond the river.

As he began to ride back to the farm the mood of pride and delight continued: his pony, his world, his time to use as he liked. He smoothed his hand down the pony's neck. The long muscles rippled like a strong current of water under his hand and he felt a sudden impulse to gallop. He took a quick look behind him and then let the pony go across the broad field, that was shut away from the farm-house by the spinneys. He dug his knees hard into the flanks and held the halter grimly with both hands and it seemed as if the response of the horse were electric. He's got racing blood all right, he thought. He's got it. He's a masterpiece, a wonder. The morning air was warm already as it rushed past his face and he saw the ground skidding dangerously away from him as the pony rose to the slope, his heart panting deeply as they reached the hurdle by the spinney, the beauty and exhilaration of speed exciting him down to the extreme tips of his limbs.

He dismounted at the hurdle and walked the rest of the way up to the house, past cart-sheds and stacks and into the little rect-angular farm-yard flanked by pig-sties and hen-houses. He led the

horse with a kind of indifferent sedateness: the idea being innocence. 'Don't you let that boy gallop that horse—you want to break
his neck?' he remembered his Aunt Bishop's words, and then his
Uncle Bishop's—'She says if you gallop him again she'll warm you
and pack you back home.' But as he led the pony over to the stables
there was no warning shout from anybody or anywhere. The yard
was dead quiet, dung-steeped and drowsy already with sun, the
pigs silent.

Suddenly, this deep silence seemed ominous.

He stopped by the stable door. Now, from the far side of the
yard, from behind the hen-houses, he could hear voices. They
seemed to be strange voices. They seemed to be arguing about
something. Not understanding it, he listened for a moment
and then tied the pony to the stable door and went across the
yard.

'Th'aint bin a fox yit as could unscrew the side of a hen-place and
walk out wi' the hens under his arm. So don't try and tell me they
is.'

'Oh! What's this then? Ain't they fox-marks? Just by your feet
there? Plain as daylight.'

'No, they ain't. Them are dug prints. I know dug prints when
I see 'em.'

'Yis, an' I know fox prints. I seen 'em afore.'

'When?'

'Over at Jim Harris's place. When they lost that lot o' hens
last Michaelmas. That was a fox all right, and so was this, I
tell y'.'

'Yis? I tell y' if this was a fox it was a two-legged 'un. Thass
what it was.'

Alexander stood by the corner of the hen-roost, listening, his
mouth open. Three men were arguing: his Uncle Bishop, limbs
as fat as bladders of lard in his shining trousers, a policeman in plain
clothes, braces showing from under his open sports jacket, police
boots gleaming from under police trousers, and Maxie, the cow-
man, a cunning little man with small rivet eyes and a striped
celluloid collar fixed with a brass stud and no tie.

It was Maxie who said: 'Fox? If that was a fox I'm a bloody
cart-horse. Ain't a fox as ever took twenty hens in one night.'

'Only a two-legged fox,' Uncle Bishop said.

'Oh, ain't they?' the policeman said.

'No, they ain't,' Uncle Bishop said, 'and I want summat done.'

'Well,' the policeman said, 'jist as you like, jist as you like. Have it your own way. I'll git back to breakfast now and be back in an hour and do me measurin' up. But if you be ruled by me you'll sit up with a gun tonight.'

II

An hour later that morning Alexander sat on a wooden bin in the little hovel next to the stable where corn was kept for the hens and pollard for the pigs, and Maxie sat on another bin, thumb on cold bacon and bread, jack-knife upraised, having his breakfast.

'Yis, boy,' Maxie said, 'it's a two-legged fox or else my old woman's a Dutchman, and she ain't. It's a two-legged fox and we're goin' to get it. Tonight.'

'How?'

'We're jis goin' wait,' Maxie said, 'jis goin' wait wi' a coupla guns. Thass all. And whoever it is 'll git oles blown in 'is trousis.'

'Supposing he don't come tonight?'

'Then we're goin' wait till he does come. We'll wait till bull's noon.'

Maxie took a large piece of cold grey-red bacon on the end of his knife and with it a large piece of bread and put them both into his mouth. His little eyes bulged and stared like a hare's and something in his throat waggled up and down like an imprisoned frog. Alexander stared, fascinated, and said 'You think you know who it is, Maxie?'

Maxie did not answer. He took up his beer-bottle, slowly unscrewed the stopper and wiped the top with his sleeve. He had the bland, secretive air of a man who has a miracle up his sleeve. His eyes, smaller now, were cocked at the distant dark cobwebs in the corner of the little hut. 'I ain't sayin' I know. An' I ain't sayin' I don't know.'

'But you've got an idea?'

Maxie tilted the bottle, closed his little weasel mouth over the top and the frog took a series of prolonged jumps in his throat. It was silent in the little hut while he drank, but outside the day was fully awake, the mist cleared away, the cuckoos in the spinney and down through the fields warmed into stuttering excitement of sun, the blackbirds rich and mad in the long hedge of pink-fading hawthorn dividing the road from the house. The boy felt a deep sense of excitement and secrecy in both sound and silence, and leaned forward to Maxie.

'I won't tell, Maxie. I'll keep it. I won't tell.'

'Skin y-alive if you do.'

'I won't tell.'

'Well,' Maxie said. He speared bread and bacon with his knife, held it aloft, and the boy waited in fascination and wonder. 'No doubt about it,' Maxie said. 'Gippos.'

'Does Uncle Bishop think it's gippos?'

'Yis,' Maxie said. 'Thinks like me. We know dug prints when we see 'em and we know fox-prints. And we know gippo prints.'

'You think it's Shako?'

'Th' ain't no more gippos about here,' Maxie said, 'only Shako and his lot.' He suddenly began to wave the knife at the boy, losing patience. 'Y' Uncle Bishop's too easy, boy. Too easy. Let's 'em do what they like, don't he? Lets 'em have that field down by the brook don't he and don't charge nothing? Lets 'em leave a cart here when they move round and don't wanta to be bothered with too much clutter. Lets 'em come here cadgin'. Don't he? Mite o' straw, a few turnips, sack o' taters, anything. Don't he?'

'Yes.'

'Well, you see where it gits 'im! Twenty hens gone in one night.' Maxie got up, sharp snappy little voice like a terrier's, the back of his hand screwing crumbs and drink from his mouth. 'But if I have my way it's gone far enough. I'll blow enough holes in Shako's behind to turn him into a bloody colander.'

Maxie went out of the hut into the sunshine, the boy following him.

'You never see nothin' funny down in the field when you went to fetch Snowy, did you? No gates left open? No hen feathers about nowhere?'

'No. It was too misty to see.'

'Well, you keep your eyes open. Very like you'll see summat yit.'

Maxie moved over towards the stables. Alexander, fretted suddenly by wild ideas, inspired by Maxie's words, went with him. 'Your going to need Snowy this afternoon, Maxie?' he said.

'Well, I'm goin' to use him this morning to git a load or two o' faggots for a stack-bottom. Oughta be finished be dinner.'

Maxie opened the lower half of the stable door. 'Look a that,' he said. The stable-pin had worked loose from its socket, the door was scarred by yellow slashes of hoofs. 'Done that yesterday,' Maxie said. 'One day he'll kick the damn door down.'

'He kicks that bottom fence like that. Kicks it to bits nearly every night.'

'Yis, I know. Allus looks to me as if he's got too much energy. Wants to be kickin' and runnin' all the time.'

'Do you think he was ever a race-horse?' Alexander said.

'Doubt it,' Maxie said. 'But he's good. He's got breedin'. Look at how he stan's. Look at it.'

The boy looked lovingly at the horse. It was a joy to see him there, white and almost translucent in the darkness of the stable, the head motionless and well up, the black beautiful eyes alone moving under the tickling of a solitary fly. He put one hand on the staunch smooth flank with a manly and important gesture of love and possession, and in that instant all the wild ideas in his mind crystallized into a proper purpose. He was so excited by that purpose that he hardly listened to Maxie saying something about 'Well, it's no use, I gotta get harnessed up and doing something,' his own words of departure so vague and sudden that he scarcely knew he had spoken them, 'I'm going now, Maxie. Going to look for a pudden' bag's nest down the brook,' Maxie's answer only reaching him after he was out in the sunshine again, 'Bit late for a pudden-bag's, ain't it? and even then not meaning anything.

He left the farm by the way he had come into it an hour or two before with the horse, going down by the stone track into the long field that sloped away to the brook and farther on to the river. It was hot now, the sky blue and silky, and he could see the heat dancing on the distances. As he went lower and lower down the slope, under the shelter of the big hawthorns and ashes and wind-beaten willows, the buttercups powdering his boots with a deep lemon dust of pollen, he felt himself sucked down by the luxuriance of summer into a world that seemed to belong to no one but himself. It gave a great sense of secrecy to what he was about to do. Farther down the slope the grasses were breast high and the path went through a narrow spinney of ash and poplar and flower-tousled elders on the fringe of it and a floor of dead bluebells, bringing him out at the other side on the crest of a short stone cliff, once a quarry face, with a grass road and the brook itself flowing along in the hollow underneath.

He went cautiously out of the spinney and behind a large hawthorn that had already shed its flowers like drifts of washed pink and orange confetti, lay down on his belly. He could see on the old grass road directly below, the gipsy camp: the round yellow varnished caravan, a couple of disused prams, washing spread on the grass, a black mare hobbled and grazing on the brook edge, a fire slowly eating a grey white hole in the bright grass. He took it in without any great excitement, as something he had seen before. What excited him were the things he couldn't see.

The trap wasn't there, and the strong brown little cob that went with it. The women weren't there. More important still, there was no sign of Shako and the men. There was no sign of life except the mare and the washing on the grass. Although he lay with his heart pumping madly into the grass it was all as he had expected it, as he hoped it would be. He took the signs of suspicion and fused them by the heat of momentary excitement into a conviction of Shako's guilt.

He waited for a long time, the sun hot on his back and the back of his neck, for something to happen. But almost nothing moved in the hollow below him except the mare taking limping steps along the brook-side, working her way into a shade, and a solitary kingfisher swooping up the brook and then sometime afterwards down again, a blue electric message sparking in and out of the over-hanging leaves.

It was almost half an hour later when he slipped quietly down the short grass of the slope between the stunted bushes of seedling hawthorn and the ledges of overhanging rock, warm as new eggs on the palm of his hand as he rested his weight on them. He went cautiously and, though his whole body was beating excitement, with that air of indifferent innocence he had used back in the farm-yard. Down in the camp he saw that the fire, almost out now, must have been lighted hours before. He put his hand on an iron-grey shirt of Shakos lying on the ground in the sun. It was so dry that it seemed to lie stiffly perched on the tops of the buttercup stems. Then he saw something else. It startled him so much that he felt his head rock faintly in the sun.

On the grass, among many new prints of horses' hoofs, lay odd lumps of grey-green hen dung. He turned one over with his dust-yellow boots. It was fresh and soft. Then suddenly he thought of something else: feathers. He began to walk about, his eyes search-ing the grass, his excitement and the heat in the sheltered hollow making him almost sick. He had hardly moved a dozen yards when he heard a shout. 'Hi! Hi'yup!' It came from the far bank of the brook and it came with a shrill unexpectedness that made his heart go off like a trap.

He stood very still, scared, waiting. He saw the elder branches on the bank of the brook stir and shake apart. He felt a second of intense fear, then another of intense relief.

Coming up from the brook was young Shako: the boy of his own age, in man's cap and long trousers braced up with binder string, eyes deep and bright as blackberries in the sun, coal-coloured hair hanging in bobtail curls in his neck.

'Hi! What you doin'?' He had a flat osier basket of watercresses in his hand.

'Looking for you,' Alexander said. 'Thought there was nobody here.'

'Lookin' for me?'

Alexander's fear seemed to evaporate through his mouth, leaving his tongue queer and dry. He and young Shako knew each other. Young Shako had often been up at the farm; once they had tried fishing for young silver trout no bigger than teaspoons in the upper reaches of the stream. Shako had seen Snowy too.

'Yes,' Alexander said. 'When're you coming for a ride with the cob and me and Snowy? You reckoned you'd come this week.'

'Won't be today,' young Shako said. 'The cob ain' here.'

'Where's he gone?' Alexander said. 'Where's everybody?'

'Old Gal's hawkin' down in Ferrers. Dad and Charley and Plum gone over to Huntingdon.'

'Long way.'

'Ain't nothing,' young Shako said. 'Jis skipped over about some ducks.'

'Ducks?'

'Selling some ducks or summat.'

Young Shako sat down on the grass, Alexander with him, careless, as though he knew nothing and nothing had happened. Ducks? Ducks was funny. He lay on the grass, some inner part of himself alert and listening. Ducks was very funny.

'You said we'd have a race,' he said. 'You on the cob and me on Snowy.'

'Cob'd eat 'im.'

'Who would? What would?' Alexander said. 'Snowy's been a race-horse.'

'Well, so's the cob. We bought 'im from a jockey-fella. Out at Newmarket. Jockey fella named Adams. Best jockey in England. You heard of 'im ain' y'?'

'Yes, but what's that? Snowy's a real race-horse. You can see it. Some hunters came by the other day and he nearly went mad. He can smell the difference in horses. Besides, we know he's been a race-horse. Ask Maxie. He's got his pedigree.'

'Pedigree? What the blarming oojah?' young Shako said. 'That's nothing. You know what a pedigree is?'

'Yes.'

'What is it?'

'Well, it's what he is. What he's been.'

'What the blarming oojah?' Shako said. 'It's summat wrong with 'is legs. Any fool knows that. Pedigree—any fool knows it's summat wrong wi' his legs.'

Alexander sat silent, almost defeated, then coming back again.

'You're frightened to race, that's all. Make out the cob's gone to Huntingdon because you daren't race.'

'Frit?' Shako said. 'Who's frit? I'll race y' any day. Any time.'

'All right. Tomorrow,' Alexander said.

'No.'

'See. I told you. Daren't.'

'What the blarming oojah! They ain't goin' be back from Huntingdon till Friday.'

Alexander stared at the sky, indifferent.

'What time did they go?' he said.

'Middle o' the night sometime,' young Shako said. 'They were gone when I got up.'

They lay for a little while longer on the grass, talking, young Shako trying to talk of big two-pound trout seen farther downstream, in the still golden hollows of the backwater where the mill had been, but the mind of Alexander could not concentrate and he had eyes for nothing except the tiniest of sand-coloured hen feathers clinging like extra petals to the edges of flowers and grass, suddenly visible because he could see them horizontally, a hen's-eye view—the same pale creamy-brown feathers that he sometimes found stuck by blood to the eggs that he collected morning and evening from the orange-boxes in the hen-roost at the farm. When he saw them, realizing fully what they meant, he lost track of what Shako was saying altogether. He got to his feet and made some excuse about going back to the farm. Shako got to his feet too, saying, 'Yis, I gotta meet the old woman and hawk this cress,' his deep black eyes careless and tired and Spaniard-like in the full sun, his voice calling Alexander back from the dozen paces he had taken across the field.

'You wanna race Friday I'll race you if they're back. If they ain't back I'll race you Saturday.'

'All right.' In that second Alexander came to his senses. 'I'll come down and see when they are back,' he said.

He made the climb back up the slope, over the warm projecting rocks and up through the spinney and into the warm security of the breast-high grasses beyond it in a state of such excitement that he could not think or speak to himself. He could only beat his hands like drumsticks on his brown bare knees in a tattoo of triumph and delight.

III

That night he knew that his Uncle Bishop and Maxie sat up in the farm-yard with loaded guns, Maxie in the little corn-hovel, his uncle under the cart-shed, from somewhere about midnight to the first colour of daylight about three o'clock, waiting for Shako. In the small back bedroom where in autumn and winter the long brown-papered trays of apples and pears would be laid out under his bed and over every inch of the cold linoleum of the floor, so that there was a good excuse for never kneeling to say his prayers, he kept awake for a long time, listening for something to happen, yet hoping and really knowing it wouldn't happen, suddenly falling asleep in a moment when as it were he wasn't looking, and waking an hour too late to fetch Snowy from the field.

Of what had happened down at the brook with young Shako he did not say a word all that day, Thursday, and all the next. He heard more talk of two-legged foxes, talked to Maxie himself of the way the men had sat up listening and waiting and hearing nothing but the sound of Snowy kicking the fences over the dead quiet fields. He saw the constable come into the yard again, making a pretence of taking measurements, arguing, really whiling away, as Maxie said, the bleedin' government's time and doing nothing. He knew that his Uncle and Maxie sat up that night again, waiting for a Shako that he alone knew would not come, and he let it happen partly out of a queer impulse of secrecy and partly because of a fear that no one would ever believe his simple and exciting piece of detective fantasy.

It was Friday afternoon when he rode Snowy down the track by the spinney and out across the buttercup field and down to the edge of the quarry. He sat bare-back, the only way he knew how to ride, and the warm sweat of a canter in the hot sun across the shadeless field broke out on his legs and seemed to glue him to the pony. The delight of being alone, in the heat and silence of a mid-summer afternoon that seemed to grow more and more intense as the ripe grasses deepened about the pony's legs like dusty wheat, was something he loved and could hardly bear. The may-blossom was over now, like cream soured and gone in the sun, and elderberry had taken its place, sweet-sour itself, the summery vanilla odour putting the whole sheltered hollow to sleep. So that as he halted Snowy and called down to the camp to young Shako, who was lying alone in the grass by the side of the hobbled little brown cob, his voice was like the sudden cracking of a cup in the stillness.

'Ready to race?'

'Eh?'

Young Shako turned sharply and rolled to his feet like a black untidy puppy, blinking in the sun.

'Now?' he called back.

'It's Friday!' Alexander said. 'You said Friday.'

'Right-o! Wait'll I git the cob.'

Young Shako began to untie the rope hobbling the cob's fore-legs, but Alexander was no longer looking at him. The camp was deserted again except for the cob and the boy, but down under the caravan Alexander could see suddenly a white-washed crate, an empty hen-crate. It startled and excited him so much that he hardly realized that young Shako was ready and already calling his name.

'Hiyup! You go along the top and I'll go along the bottom and meet you!'

'Right-o!'

Alexander turned the white pony and almost simultaneously young Shako scrambled belly-wise on the cob's back and turned him in the same direction along the brookside. They rode along together, hoofs making no noise in the thick grass, the excitement of silence beating deeply in the boy's breast and throat. It seemed to him too that Snowy was excited, sensing something. His head seemed exceptionally high up, splendid in the sun with a sort of alert nobility, his beauty and strength flowing out to the boy, so that he felt outlandishly proud and strong himself.

Gradually the quarry-face shallowed down until the land was entirely on one level. Alexander halted Snowy and waited for young Shako to come up to him. The land had begun to be broken up by sedge and to Alexander it looked as though the cob, strug-gling between the stiff rushes and ground bubbled by ant-hills, was ugly and ordinary and short-winded. Until that moment the boys had not spoken again, but now Shako said where were they going to race? Up on the top field above the marsh? and Alexander said, 'Yes, up in the top field,' and they rode the horses away from the brook together, skirting the marsh where even the high spears of reed were dead still in the windless afternoon, blades of dark green steel sharp in the sun above the torches of lemon iris and islands of emerald grass among the fly-freckled pools.

'So they got back from Huntingdon?' Alexander said.

'Yeh! Got back. Got back late last night.'

'Gone somewhere today?'

'Only down to the market. Be back any time now.'

'How far are we going to race?'

'Far as you like.'

'Make it from the fence over to the first sycamore, shall we?' Alexander said.

'Ain't very far.'

'All right. Make it from the fence over to the feed-trough. That's a good way.'

'All right,' Shako said. 'Anybody who falls off loses.'

The sun beat down on them strongly as they turned up the field to meet it. Snowy lifted his head and Alexander could feel in him a sudden excited vibration of strength. His own heart was beating with such deep sickness that as they reached the fences and turned the horses he could not speak. He sat tense and silent, his senses cancelled out by the suspense of excitement. In this moment the world too was cancelled out except for the dazzling blaze of buttercups and the poised chalk statue of Snowy's head and the murmur of grasshoppers breaking and carrying away the silence on tremulous and infinite waves of sound.

Another second and young Shako counted three and lifted his hand and dropped it and Alexander did not know anything except that something amazing and unearthly happened to Snowy. He became something tearing its way off the golden rim of the earth. He felt him to be like a great white hare bouncing madly into space. He leaned forward and clung to his neck, frightened of falling or being thrown. The sycamore trees sailed past like balloons broken adrift and five seconds later he saw the two stone feed-troughs flash past him like boats torn from their moorings too.

Snowy did not come to a standstill until they reached the hedge and the end of the field. He stood for a moment fretting and panting deeply. It had been like a burst of majestic fury. It filled Alexander with a pride and astonishment that momentarily took his speech away, so that as he turned and saw young Shako and the cob clumsily pulling up at the troughs he could not speak.

He walked Snowy slowly back. His pride was one with the pony's, deep, quiet, almost dignified. It sprang out of the pony's heart. It stirred him to a few seconds of such love for the horse that he suddenly dismounted and seized his warm dribbling head in his hands.

'You see, I told you,' he said to Shako at last. 'He's been a race-horse.'

'Wadn't much,' Shako said. The deep Spaniard eyes were prouder in defeat than Alexander's were in triumph. 'Cob was just tired after that long journey from Huntingdon. Bet y' I'd race you tomorrow and win y' easy. What y' goin' be up to now? Going home?'

Alexander remembered how old Shako and his brothers Plum and Charley must be back from market soon, perhaps now, already.

'No,' he said, 'I'll come back a bit with you. Cool Snowy off and perhaps give him a drink.'

'Don't wanna give him no drink while he's so ragin' hot.'

'No, I know that. I'll just walk steady back with you. I want a drink myself.'

They walked back down the field towards the stream, not saying much. Snowy was oily with sweat and the heat caught Alexander in the nape of the neck like a blow as they came into the sheltered ground beyond the quarry.

It was at that moment he saw that old Shako and Plum and Charley were back, one of the women with them. He saw the flare of the woman's yellow blouse and the dark beet-red skirt. The men were gaunt, hungry as hawks, shifty, with untranslatable darkness behind the friendliness of their eyes.

'Young Bish!' old Shako said. He grinned with white eager teeth. 'Thass nice pony you got. Fus' time I see him.'

'Nice pony,' Shako's brothers said.

The three men came round the horse, laying long dark hands on the white flanks.

'Nice pony.' Old Shako looked at Snowy's mouth, and Alexander felt proud that Snowy stood so still and lovably dignified.

'Nice pony. On'y thing is he's gettin' old,' Shako said. 'Been about awhile.'

'Nice pony though,' Charley said.

'Yis. Nice pony,' Shako said. 'You wanna look after him. Be gettin' 'im pinched else. Nice pony like that.'

The dark hands were smoothed on the white flanks again, and it seemed suddenly to Alexander that they might be hands of possession. His fears were suddenly heightened by something Shako said. 'Knew a man once, Cakey Smith, he had a white horse and got it pinched. Somebody painted it black. Right, ain't it, Charley?'

'Right,' Charley said.

Alexander did not speak. He knew that they were kidding him. He saw sparks of lying winks flash out of Shako's eyes, but he was suddenly frightened. He got hold of Snowy's bridle and prepared to lead him away and all at once the woman's voice came singsonging from the caravan:

'Oh! the boy's lucky. Got a lucky face all right. Got a lucky face. Nobody'll pinch nothing from him. A lucky nice face he's got. Lucky. He'll be all right.'

'Well, so long,' Alexander said.

'So long,' young Shako said. 'Race y' tomorrow if y' want.'

Suddenly Alexander's wits came back. He remembered why he was here, what it was all about. He remembered what his wild plan had been.

'I can't come tomorrow,' he said. 'Not Saturday.' He felt new sweat break and flush his face as he told the lie. 'We're going out. All of us. Over to Aunt Tilda's for the night. Going tomorrow afternoon and not coming back till Sunday.'

'Lucky boy,' the woman said. 'Oh! You're a lucky boy.'

He walked away with her voice following him calling him lucky, and feeling the sombre eyes of the men swivelling after him. Once up the slope and beyond the spinney he could not walk fast enough. He stopped Snowy by a fence and got on his back. He rode up the track under a deep impulse of excitement and an imagination flared by the behaviour of Snowy and the gipsies and all he had heard.

He rode into the farmyard to put up the basking hens in a scared squawking clutter of brown and white wings. He leapt off the horse and felt the terrific excitement of a kind of heroism as he ran into the house, knowing that the time had come when he could keep things to himself no longer, knowing that he had to tell somebody now.

IV

The following night, Saturday, Alexander lay in the little iron bedstead in the apple bedroom with his trousers on and his boots in readiness under the bed. 'No!' Aunt Bishop had said, 'they ain't goin' to sit up for no fox and no nothing else, so there! And even if they was you'd get to bed and get your sleep just the same. So don't whittle your belly about that!'

Very excited, he lay listening for a long time in the warm darkness of the little room. Twice he got up and stood at the window and looked out, smelling the summer night, seeing nothing to break the colour of darkness except the rosy-orange flowering of distant iron-ore furnaces on the hills beyond the river, hearing nothing to break the sound except a momentary lift of breeze stirring the pear-leaves on the house-wall under the window. For long periods he sat up in bed, eyes wide open so that they should not close altogether, and once he got up and, for the first time in his life, voluntarily washed his face. The cold water woke him afresh and after what seemed to him hours he heard the twang-clanging of the American clock, with the view of Philadelphia 1867, being wound by his Aunt Bishop in the living-room below, and then her feet on the stairs and finally the latch of her bedroom door breaking one silence and beginning another.

He waited for what he felt was five minutes and then got up and put on his jacket and tied his boots round his neck. He opened the door of his room and waited, listening. His heart seemed to pound at the darkness. He knew that the stairs creaked at every step and finally he lay on the banisters and slid down with no sound but a faint snake-like slither. The kitchen door was unlocked and he went out that way, sitting on the door-mat to put on his boots.

In the darkness his senses were so sharpened by excitement that he could feel the presence of his Uncle Bishop and Maxie before he heard the whispers of their voices. They were sitting together under the cart-shed. For a minute he did not know what to do. Then he remembered the warm kindly face of his Uncle Bishop and the favourite phrase of his aunt, 'Can't see nothing wrong in that boy, can you? I don' know! You'd give him your head if he asked for it,' and he ran suddenly across the stack-yard, calling in a whisper who he was. 'It's all right, it's me, it's Alexander,' his heart bumping with guilt and excitement.

'Be God, you'll git me hung,' his Uncle Bishop said.

'Lucky for you y'aint in Kingdom Come,' Maxie said. 'I was half a mind to shoot.'

'Young gallus!' his uncle said. 'Frightening folks to death.'

'Can I stop?' Alexander said.

'Looks as y're stopping,' Maxie said. 'Jis be quiet. Y' oughta ding 'is ear,' he said to Uncle Bishop. 'Too soft with 'im be 'arf.'

'I told you they were coming,' Alexander said.

'We don' know as they are coming,' Maxie said, 'yit.'

For a long time nobody spoke again. The fields were dead silent all round the house and when Alexander looked out from the hovel he was so excited that he felt that the stars swung in their courses over the straw-stacks and the trees. His hands trembled and he pressed them between his knees to quieten them. And then he heard something. It startled him by its closeness and familiarity: the clopping of Snowy's hoofs on the ground.

'Where's Snowy?' he said.

'In the stable,' Maxie said. 'We shut him up so's they should think we'd really gone. See?'

'Diddling 'em?'

'Diddlin' 'em,' Maxie said. 'Gotta be artful wi' gippos. Else they diddle you.'

They sat silent for a long time again, the night broken by no sound except the occasional clop of Snowy's hoofs and a brief whisking of wind stirring into the stacks and sometimes an odd sleepy murmur from the hens. A sort of drugged suspense took hold of Alexander, so that once he lost count of time and place and himself, as though he were asleep on his feet.

It was Maxie's voice that sprung him back to full consciousness and excitement. 'Ain't that somebody moochin' about behind the pig-sties?'

'Somebody or summat round there. Them 'ugs ain't rootlin' up for nothing.'

'Listen! Somebody's comin' up round the back.'

Alexander and the two men sat tense, waiting. The boy could hear the sound of someone moving in the deep nettles and grass behind the pig-sties. The sound came nearer, was in the yard itself, was translated suddenly into moving figures. Maxie moved out of the hovel. The boy knelt on his hands and knees, clawing with his finger nails at a flint embedded in the dry earth, loosening it at last and weighing it in his hand. He felt astonishingly brave and angry and excited. Down across the yard there was a sound of wood being gently splintered: of the plank, as before, being prised out of the side of the locked hen-house. As he heard it he felt the pressure of his Uncle Bishop's hand against his chest, forcing him back a pace or two into the cart-shed. As he moved back he caught his heel against the lowered shaft of the pony cart and slipped. He groped wildly and fell against the side of the shed, the impact clattering the loose corrugated iron roof like a tin skeleton.

When he picked himself up again Maxie and his uncle were already running across the yard, shouting. He began running too. Somebody was slashing a way out through the nettles behind the pig-sties, out towards the orchard. The sows had woken up and were thundering against the sty-doors and the hens had set up a wild cluttering of terror. Alexander flung the flint wildly in the darkness. It hit the iron roof of the pig-sties like a huge explosive cap going off and the next moment, at the gate of the orchard, Maxie fired a shot. For a moment Alexander felt that he had been knocked off his feet. The shot seemed to reverberate across half the world, the boomerang of echoes came smashing back and stirred cattle and hens and pigs to hysteria in which he too was yelling madly.

He was half way across the orchard, Maxie in front, his Uncle Bishop waddling behind, the gippos already lost somewhere beyond the farthest trees, when he realized that there was a new sound of hysteria in the yard behind him. He stopped, and knew suddenly that it was Snowy, kicking the stable down.

He ran straight back, seeing better now in the darkness but still blundering against low branches of fruit-trees, barking his shins on pig-troughs in the stack-yard, brushing past the fat outspread arms of his Uncle Bishop, yelling at him to come. As he reached the stack-yard, mounting straight over the muck-hill, he heard the crack of the stable-door as it split the staple and the final frenzied hammering of Snowy's hoofs as they beat back the swinging door again and again until Snowy himself was free. The horse swung out of the dark hole of the stable like the ghost of a flying horse on a roundabout, circling wildly out of sight behind the far stacks, making drivelling noises of terror. The boy ran to and fro in the dark yard like someone demented himself, calling his uncle, then Maxie.

'Be God, what the nation is it? Boy, what is it? Boy, wheer the devil are y'?'

'It's Snowy!' he yelled. 'Maxie! It's Snowy. It's Snowy. Maxie! Uncle!'

He was almost crying now. The men were rushing about the yard. His Aunt Bishop, from an upstairs window, was shouting incomprehensible threats or questions or advice, no one listening to her.

They were listening only to Alexander, to what he had to say. 'Which way did he go, boy? Did you see him go? Which way?' And when he had nothing to say except 'I saw him go by the stacks,

that's all', they stood listening to a sound coming from far down
the road, and he stood listening with them, his heart very scared,
fear and excitement beating his brain dizzy.

It was a sound like the noise of a tune played on handbones:
the sound of Snowy galloping on the road, far away already towards the river.

v

By nine o'clock on Sunday morning the three of them, Uncle
Bishop and Maxie with Alexander riding on the carrier of Maxie's
bicycle, had reached a point where the brook ran over the road,
under a white hand-rail bridge between an arch of alders, four
miles upstream. Zig-zagging across the countryside, they had been
riding and walking since six o'clock, asking everyone they met, a
shepherd with his dog, a parson out walking before breakfast,
labourers, a tramp or two: 'Y' ain't seen a white horse nowhere?
Got out last night. Ain't got no bridle on nor nothing', but no one
had seen him and Alexander's heart had begun to curl up like a
small tired animal on the verge of sickness.

A small hill, not much more than a green breastwork, curved
up from one side of the brook, and Maxie clambered up it on thick
squat legs to take a squint over the surrounding land. He came down
shaking his head, pressing tired heels in the slope. Sun hit the bub-
bling surface of the water as it lippled over the road, the dazzling
quicksilver light flashing back in Alexander's eyes, making him
tired too.

'No sign on 'im,' Maxie said. 'No tellin' wheer he is got to. Rate
he was runnin' he'll very like be half-way round England.'

'More likely busted isself up on something. On a fence or something, barbed wire or something,' Uncle Bishop said.

'Well,' Maxie said, 'ain't no use stannin' about. Let's get on as
far as Shelton. We can ask Fat Sturman if he's seed 'im.'

'Fat Sturman?' Uncle Bishop said. 'It's Sunday morning. He
won't be able to tell a white horse from a black for another twenty-
four hours. Allus sozzled Saddays and Sundays, you know that.

'I forgot,' Maxie said. 'Well, we can ask somebody. Ask the fust
man we meet.'

They walked despondently up the hill, pushing the bicycles. It
was hot and silent everywhere, bees thick in the grass, the flat
empty Sunday morning stillness seeming to Alexander to stretch
far over the quivering horizon. Climbing, he looked at his boots.

The lace-holes looked back at him from the pollen-yellow leather with the sad stoical eyes of Chinamen.

When he looked up again he was surprised to see an oldish woman coming down the hill, walking in a prim lardidardy way as though she had springs in the heels of her flat cloth-sided boots. On the top of an ant-hill of grey hair she had a huge fruit basket of a hat that reminded him of the glass-case of artificial grapes and pears and cherries that stood on the bible in his Aunt Bishop's parlour. The woman was carrying a prayer-book in her hands and Alexander could see her turning to smile at the trees as she went past, as though she had hidden friends in them.

'Shall we ask her?' Uncle Bishop whispered.

'Won't know a horse from a dead donkey,' Maxie said.

'Never know,' Uncle Bishop said. 'Way she's bouncing down the hill she might a bin a jockey.'

'Well, you ask her. Not me.'

Half a minute later Uncle Bishop had taken off his hat and was making a little speech in a strange aristocratic voice to the old lady, who stood with hands clasped over the prayer-book, smiling with a kind of saintly beatitude. 'Hexcuse me, madam, but hi suppose you hain't seen a white pony nowheer? Hescaped last night. Much hobliged lady, if you seen hany sign of 'im.'

The old lady took one smiling, saintly look at the two men and Alexander.

'Yes,' she said, 'I have.'

'My God,' Maxie said, 'wheer?'

The old lady looked at Maxie. 'Did you use the name of God?'

'Yis, but—'

'In front of the little boy?'

'Yis, but—'

'My man, you ought to burn in hell!'

Sheepish and exasperated and at a loss, Uncle Bishop and Maxie stood looking at the ground, not knowing what to say, and the old lady suddenly began to make a strange rambling speech of reproval, preaching decency and godliness and respect for the Sabbath, her voice by turns like vinegar and honey, one hand sometimes upraised in a little gesture to the sky, until finally Alexander could stand it no longer.

'Please,' he said, 'please tell us where the horse is. Something might have happened to him. He might be bad. He might be dying.'

'Everybody is dying,' she said.

His heart sank; tears of anger and frustration hit his eyes and sprang back. 'Tell us where he is,' he said. 'Please. Tell us where he is.'

She was still smiling, saintly, slightly but rather nicely mad, and for one second the boy did not believe a word of all she had said. Then all at once she turned and pointed up the hill.

'He's at the top of the hill. Lying on the grass. Lying under a tree.'

Maxie and Alexander and Uncle Bishop ran up the hill. 'God bless you,' the old lady called, but they scarcely heard it.

The white pony was lying as the old lady had said in the shade of an ash tree at the top of the hill. As he heard footsteps and voices he lifted his head, and a small black explosion of flies rose from one eye. The boy called his name and with a great eager effort, making odd noises in his throat, the pony tried to struggle to his feet. He made the effort and sank back and Maxie knelt down by his head. 'All right, Snowy. All right. Goo' boy. Goo' boy then. All right.'

'We got to git 'im up,' Uncle Bishop said.

'Yis,' Maxie said, 'we got to git 'im up. Stan' back, boy. Very like he'll make a bit of a to-do. Stan' back.'

Alexander stood back but the white pony could not rise. 'Come on Snowy,' the men said, 'come on now. Come on,' but nothing happened. It was cool under the ash tree but it seemed to the boy that the pony was held down by the heat of a great exhaustion. Each time he lifted his head the flies broke away in a small black explosion and then settled again.

They tried for almost half an hour to get the pony to his feet, but Maxie said at last: 'It's no good. We gotta git somebody else to look at him. You wait here and I'll bike into Shelton and git Jeff Emery. He's a knacker.'

'Knacker?' Uncle Bishop said.

'Well, he's a bit of a vet too. Does both. He'll know what to do if anybody does.'

Maxie got on his bicycle and rode away up the hill. Alexander and Uncle Bishop stood and looked at the white pony. The depth of silence seemed to increase when Maxie had gone, bees moaning in the honeysuckle and the blackberry flowers, yellow hammers chipping mournful notes on the hedgerows, a bell for morning service donging a thin hole in the distance over the hill.

'Think he'll get up?' the boy said.

'He'll get up, he's just tired. You would be if you'd galloped about all night.'

'Shako says he's old. He's not, is he?'

'He ain't young.'

'You think he's been a race-horse and the shot made him think he was in a race again?'

'I count that's what it was.' Uncle Bishop took another look at the pony. 'Well, it's no good. I gotta see a man about a dog. You comin'?' and he and Alexander went and stood over by the far hedge. 'Hedge-roses out nice,' Uncle Bishop said. 'Grow all the better for a little water.'

When they turned again something had happened. Very quiet and looking in some way very fragile, the white pony was on his feet. The boy's heart seemed to turn somersaults of happiness. He ran and put his hands on the pony's head, smoothing his nose, talking softly. 'Snowy. Good Snowy. Good boy, Snowy.'

'You think he's all right?' he said.

'You think he could walk as far as the brook? Perhaps he wants a drink?'

'Yeh. Let him walk if he will. Don't force him. Let him go how he likes.'

'Come on, Snowy,' the boy said. 'Come on, Snowy. Good Snowy. Good boy. Come on.'

The pony walked slowly down the hill in hot sunshine. At the bottom of the hill, where the brook ran over the road, he put his lips to the water. He let the water run into and past his mouth, not really drinking. He stood like that for a long time, not moving at all.

Suddenly he went down on his fore-legs and sank into the water. Alexander and Uncle Bishop had not time to do anything before they heard a shout and saw Maxie, with a man in breeches and leggings, coming down the hill.

'Summat we can do, Jeff, ain't there?' Maxie said. 'Summat we can do?'

The man did not answer. He knelt down by the pony, pressing his hands gently on the flanks.

'Well, there's jis' one thing we can do, that's all.'

The boy stood scared and dumb, watching the water break against the body of the horse, not seeing the men's faces.

'All right,' Maxie said. He took Alexander by the arm. 'Boy, you git hold o' my bike and take it across the bridge and put it underneath that furdest ash tree, outa the sun. I don't want the tyres bustin'.'

'Is Snowy going to be all right?' the boy said.

'Yis. He's going to be all right.'

Alexander took the bicycle and wheeled it across the bridge and along the road. The ash tree was fifty yards away. He reached it and laid the bicycle against the trunk in the shade. The bell tinkled as it touched the tree and at the same time as if the bell were a signal, he heard a sharp, dull report from the brook, and he turned in time to see the man in breeches and leggings holding a strange-looking pistol in his hand.

Running wildly back to the brook, trying to shout and not shouting, he saw the white pony's head lying flat and limp in the water. The water was lapping over the eyes, and out of the head and mouth a long scarf of blood was slowly unwinding itself downstream. The men had their backs turned away from him as though they did not want to look at him, and he knew that the white pony had gone for ever.

What he did not know until long afterwards was that there, at that moment, in the dead silence of the summer morning, with the sun blazing down on the white pony and the crimson water and the buttercups rich as paint in the grass, some part of his life had gone for ever too.

The Princess and the Puma

There had to be a king and queen, of course. The king was a terrible old man who wore six-shooters and spurs, and shouted in such a tremendous voice that the rattlers on the prairie would run into their holes under the prickly pear. Before there was a royal family they called the man 'Whispering Ben'. When he came to own 50 000 acres of land and more cattle than he could count, they called him O'Donnell 'the Cattle King'.

The queen had been a Mexican girl from Laredo. She made a good, mild wife, and even succeeded in teaching Ben to modify his voice sufficiently in the house to keep the dishes from being broken. When Ben got to be king she would sit on the gallery of Espinosa Ranch and weave rush mats. When wealth became so irresistible and oppressive that upholstered chairs and a centre table were brought down from San Antone in the wagons, she bowed her smooth, dark head, and shared the fate of the Danaë.

To avoid indiscretion you have been presented first to the king and queen. They do not enter the story, which might be called 'The Chronicle of the Princess, the Happy Thought, and the Lion that Bungled his Job'.

Josefa O'Donnell was the surviving daughter, the princess. From her mother she inherited warmth of nature and a dusky, semi-tropic beauty. From Ben O'Donnell the royal she acquired a store of intrepidity, common sense, and the faculty of ruling. The combination was one worth going miles to see. Josefa while riding her pony at a gallop could put five out of six bullets through a tomato-can swinging at the end of a string. She could play for hours with a white kitten she owned, dressing it in all manner of absurd clothes. Scorning a pencil, she could tell you out of her head what 1545 two-year-olds would bring on the hoof, at $8.50 per head. Roughly speaking, the Espinosa Ranch is forty miles long and thirty broad—but mostly leased land. Josefa, on her pony, had prospected over every mile of it. Every cow-puncher on the range knew her by sight and was a loyal vassal. Ripley Givens, foreman of one of the Espinosa outfits, saw her one day, and made up his mind to form a royal matrimonial alliance. Presumptuous? No. In those days in the Nueces country a man was a man. And, after all, the title of cattle king does not presuppose blood royal. Often it only signifies that its owner wears the crown in token of his magnificent qualities in the art of cattle stealing.

One day Ripley Givens rode over to the Double-Elm Ranch to inquire about a bunch of strayed yearlings. He was late in setting out on his return trip, and it was sundown when he struck the White Horse Crossing of the Nueces. From there to his own camp it was sixteen miles. To the Espinosa ranch-house it was twelve. Givens was tired. He decided to pass the night at the Crossing.

There was a fine water-hole in the river-bed. The banks were thickly covered with great trees, undergrown with brush. Back from the water-hole fifty yards was a stretch of curly mesquite grass—supper for his horse and bed for himself. Givens staked his horse, and spread out his saddle blankets to dry. He sat down with his back against a tree and rolled a cigarette. From somewhere in the dense timber along the river came a sudden, rageful, shivering wail. The pony danced at the end of his rope and blew a whistling snort of comprehending fear. Givens puffed at his cigarette, but he reached leisurely for his pistol-belt, which lay on the grass, and twirled the cylinder of his weapon tentatively. A great gar plunged with a loud splash into the water-hole. A little brown rabbit skipped around a bunch of cat-claw and sat twitching his whiskers and looking humorously at Givens. The pony went on eating grass.

It is well to be reasonably watchful when a Mexican lion sings soprano along the arroyos at sundown. The burden of his song may be that young calves and fat lambs are scarce, and that he has a carnivorous desire for your acquaintance.

In the grass lay an empty fruit can, cast there by some former sojourner. Givens caught sight of it with a grunt of satisfaction. In his coat pocket tied behind his saddle was a handful or two of ground coffee. Black coffee and cigarettes! What ranchero could desire more?

In two minutes he had a little fire going clearly. He started with his can, for the water-hole. When within fifteen yards of its edge he saw, between the bushes, a side-saddled pony with down-dropped reins cropping grass a little distance to his left. Just rising from her hands and knees on the brink of the water hole was Josefa O'Donnell. She had been drinking water, and she brushed the sand from the palms of her hands. Ten yards away, to her right, half concealed by a clump of sacuista, Givens saw the crouching form of the Mexican lion. His amber eyeballs glared hungrily; six feet from them was the tip of the tail stretched straight, like a pointer's. His hindquarters rocked with the motion of the cat tribe preliminary to leaping.

Givens did what he could. His six-shooter was thirty-five yards away lying on the grass. He gave a loud yell, and dashed between the lion and the princess.

The 'rucus', as Givens called it afterwards, was brief and somewhat confused. When he arrived on the line of attack he saw a dim streak in the air, and heard a couple of faint cracks. Then a hundred pounds of Mexican lion plumped down upon his head and flattened him, with a heavy jar, to the ground. He remembered calling out: 'Let up, now—no fair gouging!' and then he crawled from under the lion like a worm, with his mouth full of grass and dirt, and a big lump on the back of his head where it had struck the root of a water-elm. The lion lay motionless. Givens, feeling aggrieved, and suspicious of fouls, shook his fist at the lion, and shouted: 'I'll rastle you again for twenty——' and then he got back to himself.

Josefa was standing in her tracks, quietly reloading her silver-mounted ·38. It had not been a difficult shot. The lion's head made an easier mark than a tomato-can swinging at the end of a string. There was a provoking, teasing, maddening smile upon her mouth and in her dark eyes. The would-be rescuing knight felt the fire of his fiasco burn down to his soul. Here had been his chance, the chance that he had dreamed of; and Momus, and not Cupid, had presided over it. The satyrs in the wood were, no doubt, holding their sides in hilarious, silent laughter. There had been something like vaudeville—say Signor Givens and his funny knockabout act with the stuffed lion.

'Is that you, Mr Givens?' said Josefa, in her deliberate, saccharine contralto. 'You nearly spoiled my shot when you yelled. Did you hurt your head when you fell?'

'Oh, no,' said Givens quietly; 'that didn't hurt.' He stooped ignominiously and dragged his best Stetson hat from under the beast. It was crushed and wrinkled to a fine comedy effect. Then he knelt down and softly stroked the fierce, open-jawed head of the dead lion.

'Poor old Bill!' he exclaimed mournfully.

'What's that?' asked Josefa sharply.

'Of course you didn't know, Miss Josefa,' said Givens, with an air of one allowing magnanimity to triumph over grief. 'Nobody can blame you. I tried to save him, but I couldn't let you know in time.'

'Save who?'

'Why, Bill. I've been looking for him all day. You see, he's been our camp pet for two years. Poor old fellow, he wouldn't have hurt a cotton-tail rabbit. It'll break the boys all up when they hear about it. But you couldn't tell, of course, that Bill was just trying. to play with you.'

Josefa's black eyes burned steadily upon him. Ripley Givens met the test successfully. He stood rumpling the yellow-brown curls on his head pensively. In his eyes was regret, not unmingled with a gentle reproach. His smooth features were set to a pattern of indisputable sorrow. Josefa wavered.

'What was your pet doing here?' she asked, making a last stand. 'There's no camp near the White Horse Crossing.'

'The old rascal ran away from camp yesterday,' answered Givens readily. 'It's a wonder the coyotes didn't scare him to death. You see, Jim Webster, our horse wrangler, brought a little terrier pup into camp last week. The pup made life miserable for Bill— he used to chase him around and chew his hind legs for hours at a time. Every night when bedtime came Bill would sneak under one of the boys' blankets and sleep to keep the pup from finding him. I reckon he must have been worried pretty desperate or he wouldn't have run away. He was always afraid to get out of sight of camp.'

Josefa looked at the body of the fierce animal. Givens gently patted one of the formidable paws that could have killed a yearling calf with one blow. Slowly a red flush widened upon the dark olive face of the girl. Was it the signal of shame of the true sportsman who has brought down ignoble quarry? Her eyes grew softer, and the lowered lids drove away all their bright mockery.

'I'm very sorry,' she said humbly; 'but he looked so big, and jumped so high that——'

'Poor old Bill was hungry,' interrupted Givens, in defence of the deceased. 'We always made him jump for his supper in camp. He would lie down and roll over for a piece of meat. When he saw you he thought he was going to get something to eat from you.'

Suddenly Josefa's eyes opened wide.

'I might have shot you!' she exclaimed. 'You ran right in between. You risked your life to save your pet! That was fine, Mr Givens. I like a man who is kind to animals.'

Yes; there was even admiration in her gaze now. After all, there was a hero rising out of the ruins of the anti-climax. The look on Givens's face would have secured him a high position in the SPCA.

'I always loved 'em,' said he; 'horses, dogs, Mexican lions, cows, alligators——'

'I hate alligators,' instantly demurred Josefa; 'crawly, muddy things!'

'Did I say alligators?' said Givens. 'I meant antelopes, of course.'

Josefa's conscience drove her to make further amends. She held out her hand penitently. There was a bright, unshed drop in each of her eyes.

'Please forgive me, Mr Givens, won't you? I'm only a girl, you know, and I was frightened at first. I'm very, very sorry I shot Bill. You don't know how ashamed I feel. I wouldn't have done it for anything.'

Givens took the proffered hand. He held it for a time while he allowed the generosity of his nature to overcome his grief at the loss of Bill. At last it was clear that he had forgiven her.

'Please don't speak of it any more, Miss Josefa. 'Twas enough to frighten any young lady the way Bill looked. I'll explain it all right to the boys.'

'Are you really sure you don't hate me?' Josefa came closer to him impulsively. Her eyes were sweet—oh, sweet and pleading with gracious penitence. 'I would hate anyone who would kill my kitten. And how daring and kind of you to risk being shot when you tried to save him! How very few men would have done that!'

Victory wrested from defeat! Vaudeville turned into drama! Bravo, Ripley Givens!

It was now twilight. Of course Miss Josefa could not be allowed to ride on to the ranch-house alone. Givens resaddled his pony in spite of that animal's reproachful glances, and rode with her. Side by side they galloped across the smooth grass, the princess and the man who was kind to animals. The prairie odours of fruitful earth and delicate bloom were thick and sweet around them. Coyotes yelping over there on the hill! No fear. And yet——

Josefa rode closer. A little hand seemed to grope. Givens found it with his own. The ponies kept an even gait. The hands lingered together, and the owner of one explained—

'I never was frightened before, but just think! How terrible it would be to meet a really wild lion! Poor Bill! I'm so glad you came with me!'

O'Donnell was sitting on the ranch gallery.

'Hallo, Rip!' he shouted—'that you?'

'He rode in with me,' said Josefa. 'I lost my way and was late.'

'Much obliged,' called the cattle king. 'Stop over, Rip, and ride to camp in the morning.'

But Givens would not. He would push on to camp. There was a bunch of steers to start off on the trail at daybreak. He said good night, and trotted away.

An hour later, when the lights were out, Josefa, in her night-robe, came to her door and called to the king in his own room across the brick-paved hallway—

'Say, pop, you know that old Mexican lion they call the "Gotch-eared Devil"—the one that killed Gonzàles, Mr Martin's sheep herder, and about fifty calves on the Salado range? Well, I settled his hash this afternoon over at the White Horse Crossing. Put two balls in his head with my ·38 while he was on the jump. I knew him by the slice gone from his left ear that old Gonzales cut off with his machete. You couldn't have made a better shot yourself, daddy.'

'Bully for you,' thundered Whispering Ben from the darkness of the royal chamber.

The Unicorn

It was thanks to Mr Kandinsky that Joe knew a unicorn when he saw one.

He also knew that the Elephant and Castle was the Infanta of Castile, a Spanish princess. He knew that Moses was an Egyptian priest, that the Chinese invented fireworks, that Trotsky was the best revolutionary, and that pregnant was going to have a baby. Joe was six, and thanks to Mr Kandinsky, he was educated, although he didn't go to school, for he had to look after his mother till they came to Africa.

His father said to Joe when he was still five, 'Look after mother till you come,' and Joe said he would. Then he went down to talk to Mr Kandinsky in the basement. No teacher knew what Mr Kandinsky knew, about the Elephant and Castle, that is, and the unicorn. Soon after, Joe's father went to Africa, with two suitcases and a Madeira hat for the hot weather.

Joe lived upstairs at number 111 Fashion Street. There was a bedroom and a kitchen, and the kitchen had a fireplace and a gas stove, but no sink. The tap was at the top of the first flight of stairs, and Mr Kandinsky used it too. The lavatory was in the yard at the back and smelt of Keatings powder. Mr Kandinsky lived in a room on the ground floor, and had a workshop in the basement. The workshop had a window below ground level, and there was an iron grille over the pavement for the light to come through. In the little area outside the window were bits of newspaper and an old hat and sauce bottle, and Joe wondered how they got through the iron bars, because it was a top hat and the bottle was the tomato sauce kind with a wide bottom.

'We ought to look, Mr Kandinsky,' Joe said one day, 'because maybe there are some pound notes and sixpences mixed up with it all.'

'Joe,' replied Mr Kandinsky, 'who has pound notes or even sixpences to lose in Fashion Street?'

So the window was never open, except in the summer it was lowered a few inches at the top, and a lot of dust came into the workshop.

Mr Kandinsky was a trousers-maker. In the workshop he had a sewing-machine, and a bench with the surface all shining from where he and Shmule pressed trousers. In the fireplace were two big gas rings with two big goose irons beside them. When the cloth was soaked in a pail and spread over the trousers, and the hot goose iron pressed on top, a great cloud of steam arose. Mr Kandinsky always said it was bad for your health and the worst thing in tailoring, even bringing on the consumption. On the wall were three hooks with large brown-paper and cardboard patterns hanging on them. On the mantel were two boxes with flat pieces of white tailors' chalks in them, and hundreds of cloth patterns in books, and dozens of reels of cotton.

Mr Kandinsky had two pictures. Over his bench was a big print of a lady with her head bowed sitting on top of a large grey-green ball. Her eyes were bandaged and she was holding a broken harp. Joe thought the lady was a street musician who had been in a car accident; she was crying because her harp was broken and she couldn't live by singing any more. Mr Kandinsky looked at the picture for a while and said, 'You know, Joe, maybe you're right. But what about the ball she is sitting on?'

Joe thought it over while Mr Kandinsky hand-stitched a pair of fine worsted trousers, but in the end he had to give up. Then Mr Kandinsky told him:

'This ball is the world and this lady is Hope who is always with the world. She is blindfold because if she could see what happens she would lose hope and then where would she be? What this broken harp means, I don't know.'

'Maybe it's a bit of another painting,' Joe said.

'Maybe it is,' said Mr Kandinsky, 'who knows?'

'Who knows?' repeated Joe, because he liked the way Mr Kandinsky said things. 'Who knows?' he said again, putting his head to one side, opening his hands and trying to lift his eyebrows.

The other picture was a brown photograph of an old man with a long beard and side curls, and bushy eyebrows, and a great curved nose with curved nostrils. This was Mr Kandinsky's father. 'A pious man, Joe,' Mr Kandinsky said, 'very respected in the village, the finest coat-maker in the whole country.'

'Not a trousers-maker?' asked Joe.

'Certainly not,' said Mr Kandinsky, 'he was a great man and he would never lower himself to be a trousers-maker.'

'Why aren't you a coat-maker, Mr Kandinsky?' asked Joe.

Mr Kandinsky, who could answer all questions, replied,

'Because my wise father put me to trousers-making, thinking that Kandinsky and Son would be able to make complete suits. And you know what that means, Joe? It means bespoke tailoring—no more jobbing for other people. You can be an artist, not just a workman, somebody can send you sackcloth, you will make it up into a pair of trousers. But it was not to be. It was a dream, Joe. Never mind. Life is all dreams—dreams and work. That's all it is.'

After this talk, Joe nodded at the photograph of Reb Zadek Kandinsky when he came into the workshop. The stern eyes looked past him into the future, a lost future of Kandinsky and Son, bespoke tailors. The curved nostrils turned disdainfully away from Mr Kandinsky, the Fashion Street trousers-maker, well known in the trade, but not in the same class as his father, a master-tailor, who died cross-legged on his bench, stitching the revers of the first coat he had made in London. 'May he find his place in peace,' Mr Kandinsky said, 'that last coat was beautiful I tell you, Joe, beautiful.'

'I think your trousers are lovely, Mr Kandinsky,' Joe said, to cheer Mr Kandinsky up.

'Thank you, Joe,' he answered, 'I will make you a pair of blue serge trousers.' And he did, a real pair of trousers, with turn-ups, and a cash pocket. Everything, even proper flies.

The whole house was Mr Kandinsky's, not his, but he paid the whole rent and Joe's mother gave him ten shillings every week. He was an old friend and the arrangement was made before Joe's father went away. Mr Kandinsky could spare the room. 'I am the only Kandinsky extant—which means the last Kandinsky,' he told Joe. Joe thought how it must make you old to be the last one extant. He looked at Mr Kandinsky. He was very old but his face wasn't worn out. In fact he had much more face than Joe, and Joe wasn't extant at all, having both his mother and father as well as Mr Kandinsky. Joe kept a pet in the back-yard, a day-old chick, which sometimes lived for two or three weeks. After Mr Kandinsky told him he had no people he called his pets Kandinsky in memory of that family.

At Friday night supper, Mr Kandinsky and Joe's mother talked about Africa and Joe's father and what he was doing there and how soon Joe and his mother would go out to him.

'You know, Rebecca,' Mr Kandinsky said, 'your fried fish is not just fish—it is manna from heaven.'

'You are always paying me compliments, Mr Kandinsky,' Joe's mother said.

'And why not, Rebecca?' said Mr Kandinsky, 'you are the prettiest girl in the whole East End.'

'Girl,' said Joe's mother, and laughed, blushing so that she did indeed look quite pretty.

'Isn't she pretty, Joe?' asked Mr Kandinsky.

'I think you are pretty and nice,' Joe said to his mother, although she had stopped smiling, and her face looked sad and not so pretty.

'For how long?' she said, 'how long is anyone pretty?' Mr Kandinsky cleared his throat which meant he was going to say something important. Joe looked at him, waiting.

'You are pretty as long as someone loves you, Rebecca,' he said, 'and so many people love you that believe me you are very pretty. Look at me. I am ugly, and old, but even I am pretty when someone loves me.'

'I love you Mr Kandinsky,' Joe said. 'One morning you will look quite pretty.' Mr Kandinsky put his hand on Joe's head.

'Thank you, Joe,' he said. 'I feel a little bit prettier already. To celebrate I will have one more piece of this wonderful fish which the miracle of your mother's cooking has made as sweet as honey.' Mr Kandinsky, Joe thought, never got tired of fried fish.

'So what does he say in his letter this week?' Mr Kandinsky would ask. 'How is the Kaffir business?'

Joe's mother read parts of the letter out aloud, with Mr Kandinsky stopping her every so often by raising his hand and asking a question. Then they would discuss the matter for a few minutes before she went on reading. Sometimes they were very long letters, full of business details, five gross of steward's jackets, twenty gross denim trousers, add ten per cent for carriage costs, a hundred pound company, five pounds paid up, salesman's commission on a hundred ex-army bell tents, and so on.

These letters were full of excitement, with little stories of Kaffirs drinking their white beer and singing, or Kaffir boys met late at night marching down the street beating a drum, and Joe's father walking in the road, otherwise they would beat him up. The long excited letters had money in them. As Rebecca opened them, the corner of a five-pound note, and once a ten-pound note, and always a few pounds, would be seen. Unusual, exciting notes they were, not ordinary but African money. But others were very short. There was no message in them for Joe or Mr Kandinsky at all, and for Rebecca just a few words. These were the bad letters, and if Joe asked too many questions after they arrived, his mother's face would look at him as if she couldn't see, and if he went on asking questions, it would suddenly begin to tremble and then she would cry, hugging him and making his face wet with her tears.

In the mornings Joe's mother went to the Whitechapel Road where she worked in a millinery shop. She trimmed hats with bunches of artificial fruit and flowers, and Mr Kandinsky said she was the best and most artistic hat-trimmer in the millinery trade. Because she didn't come home until the late afternoon, Joe ate with Mr Kandinsky and Shmule at twelve o'clock, downstairs, in the workshop. Mr Kandinsky never allowed Joe's mother to leave something cooked for them.

'I am an old cook myself,' he told Joe, 'although your mother is the best cook in the world, Joe, I am not saying anything against her cooking.'

Mr Kandinsky cooked on one of the gas rings in the workshop. On one of them a big goose iron was always heating, and on the other a large cooking pot with two handles bubbled quietly all morning long. Into the pot Mr Kandinsky threw pieces of beef or a small breast of lamb, with plenty of onions and pepper and salt, and some large potatoes. Or a large marrow bone cooked with carrots, or mutton cooked with haricot beans. At quarter to twelve Joe went up to the street to the baker on the corner to buy three onion rolls. Then they all sat down with big enamel plates full of steaming stew, eating and talking. Joe liked Mr Kandinsky's cooking very much. 'The best cooks are men, Joe,' said Mr Kandinsky. 'Some men cooks get thousands of pounds from the Kings of Europe for cooking dinners no better than this.'

Mr Kandinsky talked a lot, but Shmule was often quiet. Shmule was short and broad, and very strong. He had bright red hair which curled into small flames, although after a haircut it was more like a piece of astrakhan. His skin was pale and his eyes grey, and every Saturday he spent the whole day at the gymnasium developing himself. Developing yourself was the only thing Shmule wanted to talk about, which was the reason why he said very little, because Joe was too young to develop himself much, and Mr Kandinsky was already too old. Occasionally Mr Kandinsky would bring Shmule into the conversation by saying, 'You got a new muscle to show us?'

Shmule at once took off his jacket. He rolled up his shirt-sleeves and clenched his fists and bent his elbows till large knots appeared everywhere. Sometimes he took off his shirt as well. He put his arms over his head, and enormous bands of muscle stood up on his back and chest. Joe clapped and Mr Kandinsky called Shmule

'Maccabeus,' which means 'The Hammer,' and was the name in which Smule wrestled. But once or twice Shmule tried a new muscle and though it came up a little distance it fell down straight away. Then he blushed from his forehead to his neck, and went into the corner to practise.

Shmule was going to be a wrestling champion, which meant he had to beat Louis Dalmatian, the Stepney Thrasher, Turk Robert, Bully Bason, and the dreaded Python Macklin. He didn't have to beat them all at once but even one at a time was enough, especially the dreaded Python Macklin, who had broken limbs with his powerful scissors grip. Shmule showed them the scissors. He took a chair and fought with it on the floor, twining his legs round it and pressing hard, explaining all the while, until one of the chair legs cracked and Mr Kandinsky shouted, 'The furniture he breaks up!'

'A chair I can mend,' said Shmule puffing and blowing, 'but supposing it was my leg?'

So between Shmule and Mr Kandinsky, Joe learned a great deal about the world. Though he was a bit young, Shmule taught him the position of defence and how to give an uppercut. But it was Mr Kandinsky who told Joe all about unicorns.

It was the afternoon that Joe's chick Kandinsky was found dead on its back, legs in the air, a ball of cotton wool and two matchsticks. Joe was worried because he did everything the day-old chick man in Club Row told him to do, and yet the chick died. Mr Kandinsky suggested that perhaps it could happen that Joe wasn't a natural-born chicken-raiser. Chickens just weren't his speciality. Maybe he should try a dog or a lizard, or a couple of fish. This made Joe think why not write to his father for a big animal, because naturally small animals only have small lives and naturally they lose them more easily.

Mr Kandinsky had been studying Africa in some detail since Joe's father went there, but the parts in the book about the gold mines and diamond mines were not as interesting as the chapter called the Fauna of Central Africa. He was, consequently, in an excellent position to advise Joe on the habits of larger animals.

They discussed the lion with some hope, because many cubs have been trained into good pets, but lions only eat meat, and where would they get enough to feed it? You couldn't fool a lion with vegetable stew; even Mr Kandinsky's cooking would only make it angry and then there would be trouble. The giraffe was nice, but with such a long neck, you couldn't get it in the house. A zebra is only a horse with stripes, and horses you can see any day in the street.

'Maybe,' Joe suggested, 'maybe my father could send a unicorn.'

'A unicorn is a public house,' Shmule said, looking up from a small book he was reading, *The Principles of Judo.*

'Don't show your ignorance on the subject, Shmule,' Mr Kandinsky said. Then he told Joe about unicorns.

'Every animal when it was made by the Almighty was given one extra-special present,' said Mr Kandinsky. 'The squirrel was given a wonderful tail to hold on with so he wouldn't fall from the trees; the horse was given strong fine legs so he could run fast; the lion great jaws; the elephant a trunk so he could take a shower whenever he felt like it, because an elephant is so large, how else could he keep clean? But the unicorn got the most special present of all. He was given a magic horn which could cure anything anyone was ever sick from. It could grant anybody's wish—straight off. And his horn consequently was worth £10,000 cash on sight, anywhere in the world. Don't ask me why the unicorn got this present. Someone had to get it, so why not him? Anyhow, he got it and no one else. But because of this very gift unicorns became so scarce you won't even find one in the zoo, so it is in life.

'At one time unicorns were as common as cart-horses, wherever you went in the streets you would see half a dozen. In those days no one was poor. You needed something so all right, you just reached out your hand and there it was, a glass of lemon tea, a new hat. Then, when people became poor, all the unicorns had their horns stolen and sold. You can imagine what that did to them. Could a lion live without his jaws, could a squirrel swing from the trees without his tail, could an elephant get on without a shower-bath, could I eat if I stopped making trousers? Of course not, so how could a unicorn live without his horn?

'Ah, Joe, they died in their thousands the lovely unicorns. They gathered together in dusty yards and at the bottom of those streets which lead nowhere. They nuzzled one another for comfort, and closed their eyes so as not to be reminded of what they had lost. Their fine white coats became spotted, their beautiful sleek muscles slipped away into twisted sinew. They pined, they shrank, they faded, they died, and their death was sad for they had been eaten up by poverty, swallowed in the darkness of a pit with no bottom, so that no one ever saw them again.'

Mr Kandinsky sighed as he bent to throw his cold goose iron on to the gas ring. He looked at Joe with big eyes and sighed. 'This was the pity of it, my Joe,' he said. 'The unicorns passed away, but poverty was still in the world, poverty and sickness. Strong men have wasted away, beautiful girls have grown ugly, children have been lost before they could yet walk, the unicorns are all gone and yet poverty is still here. Don't ask me why. What do I know?' He sighed again, then put his hand on Joe's shoulder, pressing so as to feel the small fine bone. 'Never mind,' he said, 'sometimes in spite of everything, a child grows well, a man goes from strength to strength, a woman's face does not fade. In the same way some unicorns must have lived. They were the clever ones. They saw how things were going and didn't waste time blaming men or cursing life, or threatening God, or any other foolishness. Instead they came forward and said to the rest, 'Listen friends. If we don't do something soon there will be no more unicorns left in the world.'

' "Be quiet," some of them shouted, "can't you see we are too unhappy to do anything."

' "Don't be blasphemous," others cried, "it's the will of God."

' "Don't interrupt us when we are crying," others said, "it is the only thing left for us to enjoy."

'But some gathered together to escape, some with hope in their hearts, some with doubt, a few with the spirit which does not care either for hope or doubt. These said, "Living means waste, but let who wants to live, live."

'One old unicorn who had been told about Africa when he was a baby had never forgotten. He told them, and to Africa they went that very night. In Africa they are today, although their terrible experiences made them careful about being seen by men, so that nowadays you don't see them so often. But they are even bigger now, and stronger even, and so fierce they fight at the drop of a hat. Without doubt, Joe,' said Mr. Kandinsky, 'without doubt, Shmule, you wrestler,' he said, 'there is absolutely no reason why there shouldn't be unicorns in Africa.'

'What do I know?' asked Shmule.

'Could I get a unicorn into the house?' Joe asked.

'A small unicorn,' Mr Kandinsky said, 'certainly. There is no reason why a small unicorn couldn't be got into the house. Would you like another spoonful, Joe?' He stirred the carrots in the sauce-pan on his gas ring so that a great cloud arose.

After Kandinsky the day-old chick died, Joe went to the animal market, because if you wanted a unicorn, the best place in the world to look for it was Club Row.

Joe had his own way of walking through the market. It made it much larger if you started in the middle where the herring women fished salted herrings out of barrels with red hands, dipped them in water and cleaned and sliced them with long thin knives. From there you walked up to Alf, the singing-bird man, then cut round the back, coming through the other end where the dogs were. But if there was something you wanted to buy it was much better to start at one end by the singing birds and walk through, looking carefully at every stall.

Alf, the singing-bird man, came to Mr Kandinsky for repairs so he knew Joe and always spoke to him, even if he was busy selling someone a canary. Alf was against day-old chicks as pets. He pulled his light brown overall coat down, pushed his cap back from his eyes and told Joe when he bought Kandinsky, 'You ain't doing that chick no favour, Joe, taking him away without his mother, alone, he doesn't know how to give a peep-peep yet, putting him in a box with a drop of water and a handful of straw. That rotten day-old chick man should be put in a box himself, the louse, selling chicks to anyone with a sixpence. A chick like this needs his mum or a special hot-box; he don't just grow up any old how any old where, he must have special care, he shouldn't catch cold.' Alf turned to a fat lady with a big grey fur round her neck. 'That canary, lady,' he said, 'is such a singer I should like to see better.'

'He don't appear to be singing much just now,' the lady said, taking a handful of potato-crisps from her bag and crunching them. 'Tweet-tweet,' she said to the canary, spitting a few little bits of potato-crisp at him, 'tweet-tweet.'

'Here, Oscar,' Alf said, because all his birds were sold with their right names on small red certificates. He whistled softly to the bird. Oscar turned his bead eyes towards Alf, listened for a moment, and then began to sing.

'Lovely,' the fat lady said, finishing the crisps and brushing her fur, 'how much for the bird?'

'That Oscar,' Alf said afterwards, 'I had him nearly a year.' And he started to whistle softly to a dark gold canary.

Near Alf's stall there was a jellied eel stand with a big enamel bowl of grey jellied eels, small bowls for portions, a large pile of lumps of bread, and three bottles of vinegar. There were also orange and black winkles in little tubs, and large pink whelks. People stood around shaking vinegar on to their eels and scooping them up with bread. A little thin man in a white muffler served them and sometimes dropped a large piece of eel on the ground. Behind the stand a very fat man with a striped apron and an Anthony Eden hat waved a ladle in his hand and shouted, 'Best eels, fresh jellied, buy 'em and try 'em, eels.' Over the stand a red, white and blue banner flapped. 'The Eel King,' it said. The King himself never served.

Opposite the Eel King was a red barrow with dark green water melons, and a white enamel table top with halves and slices of melon and a large knife. Joe pretended he couldn't make up his mind whether to buy some jellied eels or a slice of melon. He watched people eating eels and shaking vinegar on them, and then looked back at the large wide slices of red melon with glossy black seeds bursting from them.

In the end he bought a twopenny slice of melon and pretended it was jellied eels, scooping the red flesh with his teeth and saying 'Blast' and 'Bloody' when the seeds dropped to the pavement. Some of the seeds he saved so that when they were dry he could crack them between his teeth and get the thin nuts inside.

While he scraped the thick skin of the melon, Joe watched the Indian fortune teller who wore a turban and sold green, yellow and red perfume in small bottles. Whenever a woman bought a bottle of perfume the Indian looked at her strangely. 'A little moment, dear lady,' he said, 'a little moment while I look into the bowl.' He looked darkly into a large glass bowl which turned purple or orange, and sliding his hand beneath brought out a small envelope with a fortune in it; the pavement all round his stall was covered with torn envelopes. Once when the market was finished, Joe kicked his way through the empty boxes and newspapers past the Indian's stall. He saw him counting sixpences into piles, and putting them into small blue bags, but the bowl looked like an ordinary bowl for goldfish. An Indian girl who wore a long blue silk robe was packing the bottles into boxes on a barrow. When the Indian pushed the barrow away, the girl walked behind him; they went to the bottom of the street and turned away into the darkness under the railway arches, back to India.

The Sunday came when Joe had saved enough of the sixpences Mr Kandinsky gave him every week for helping in the workshop, to buy a unicorn, should one appear. Mr Kandinsky was always busy on Sunday mornings, and he hardly noticed Joe leave. He was arguing with a customer who wanted a zip fastener on his trousers, something to which Mr Kandinsky could not agree.

Joe ran quickly through the crowd to the singing-bird end of the market. Alf was talking to a budgerigar and a tall thin man with a sad face. The bird wasn't replying, but every so often the thin man said, 'It's no good, Alf—it's no good,' till at last Alf put the cage down. The bird suddenly said 'Hello' and Joe said hello back. The thin man looked sadder still and left, and Alf said, 'Talks better English than I do—hello, Joe, what are you after? No more chicks remember.'

'Do you know where I can find a unicorn, Alf?' Joe asked.

'Try down by the dogs, Joe,' Alf suggested. 'Hello,' the bird said again.

'Hello,' Joe replied and started towards the other end of the market.

On the way Mrs Quinn, the hen woman, called him over.

'Joe,' she said, 'tell your mother I'll bring the eggs over meself tomorrow.' She was holding a fat hen which squawked as an old woman pinched it and complained. 'If you don't like the bird for the love of St Patrick leave it,' shouted Mrs Quinn in Yiddish. 'So tell your mother now,' she said to Joe.

'Do you know where I can buy a unicorn, Mrs Quinn?' Joe asked.

'What do you want with heathen animals?' she answered. 'Get yourself a nice day-old chick.'

'That day-old chick man, the louse,' Joe said, 'he should be put in a box.'

'Will you leave the bird alone now?' screamed Mrs Quinn at the old woman who was still pinching its bottom.

'There's no harm,' Joe thought, 'in at least having a look at the chicks.'

At the stall, hundreds of them were running about in a large glass enclosure with a paraffin lamp in the middle of it, all squeaking like mice. When someone bought them they were put into cardboard boxes with air holes, and the squeaking became fainter. It was a pity they had such small lives.

'Another one already, cock?' asked the chick man.

'Not today, thank you,' said Joe, 'I'm not a born chick-raiser.'

'You got to know the trick of it, cock.'

'I'm going to buy a unicorn this time,' Joe said.

'You do that,' the man said, 'you do.' He bundled two dozen chicks into a box and tied it up with string.

Just about the middle of the market, near the herring women, was the fritter stall which also sold hokey-pokey ices and sarsaparilla fancy drinks. The smell rushed up so thick from the great vat of frying oil that if you stood nearby for a while you had a whole meal of fritters. The hokey-pokey man called out, 'Get your hokey-pokey, a penny a lump, the more you eat the more you jump,' but Joe hurried on. He passed the cat-lady with her basket of kittens mewing, and the long line of hutches where the rabbits were always eating. He waited for the bearded sandwich-board man to shout at him, 'The wages of sin is death, repent lest ye perish,' because he was studying to spit when he spoke. 'Sthin-death,' Joe spluttered as he hurried on.

The dog-sellers mostly stood in the gutter or against the bill-hoardings holding a puppy in each hand and one in each pocket. They didn't say anything unless you patted a pup. Then they told you he was a pedigree Irish retrieving elk-hound, his mother was a good house dog. A few of them had cages with bigger dogs in them, and one or two men just stood around with four or five dogs on leads, trying to make them stop walking round in circles and jumping at people. There were dogs with short legs and long tails, and dogs with short tails but long ears. They were all dogs all right, all yelping and barking, just dogs.

Joe walked right to the end of the dog-end of the market, hurry-ing past the man who bit off exactly at the joint dogs' tails that needed lopping, to the very last man standing by the arches under the railway. The four sixpences and four pennies in his pocket clinked and three men tried to sell him pedigree pups, but the last man stood by the dark opening of the arches without speaking. He held a large white rabbit under one arm, and in the other hand a piece of tattered string, and at the end of the string, a small uni-corn.

While Joe looked at the unicorn, a little man with three pullovers on came up and took the white rabbit. He held it up by its ears, and kicked its feet at him. Then he handed it back saying, 'Flem-ish?'

'Dutch,' the last man said.

'Thought it was Flemish,' the little man mumbled as he turned away.

'Dutch,' the man said again.

'Funny thing,' the little man mumbled, pulling his pullovers down, 'funny thing.'

People pushed past with bags of fruit and dogs and birds in cages but none of them spoke to the man. Then a tall boy came up and stared at the white rabbit for a while.

'How much?' he asked.

'Twelve and sixpence,' the last man said. 'It's Dutch.'

'Half a bar,' the boy replied.

'Done,' said the last man and handed over the rabbit. The tall boy left, talking into the rabbit's ear. The last man pulled at the string on the unicorn as Joe came up to pat its head. The unicorn licked Joe's hand.

'What if he is a bit twisted,' the man said, 'he'll grow straight in time.'

'He is a bit twisted,' Joe replied looking at the unicorn's hind legs, 'and one leg is shorter than the other at the back.'

'He's a runt all right,' the man said. 'Still.'

'How much is he?' Joe asked.

'Only five shillings,' the man said.

'Give you two shillings,' Joe said.

'Come orf it,' the man said.

'He's a bit twisted,' Joe said.

'What if he is a bit twisted,' the man replied, 'he'll grow.'

'Give you two and fourpence,' Joe said.

'Kids,' the man said. 'Kids.' He turned into the arches, the unicorn limping behind him, and Joe behind them both.

Under the arches the air smelt of smoke and horses, and footsteps and voices echoed through the smell. In the corners old men with long beards and old women with feathers stuck in their hats, all wrapped up in rags, sat on sacks talking to themselves. As Joe passed, an old man took a long draught from a bottle, and coughed. At the other end of the arches the last man began to hurry, and the unicorn tripped and skipped after him.

When Joe caught up with him the man stopped and the unicorn sat down.

'You still 'ere?' the man asked. 'Kids.'

'What will you do with him?' Joe said.

'Have him for dinner,' the man said.

'Oh,' Joe gasped.

'With a few onions,' the man said.

'How much is he?' Joe asked.

'How many more times?' the man said. 'Five shillings. He cost me that to raise.'

'If you come back with me to Mr Kandinsky at Fashion Street,' Joe said, 'he'll give you five shillings.'

'All that way?'

'And I'll give you two and fourpence as well,' Joe added.

'Give me the two and fourpence then,' the man said and Joe counted the coins into his hand.

'I don't mind leading him,' Joe said, 'if you're a bit tired.'

Back at the workshop Mr Kandinsky was fixing the zip fastener into the trousers because, after all, the customer is always right, even when he's wrong. He was talking to the baker from the corner. 'You know,' he was saying, as Joe came in leading the unicorn, 'the black bread agrees with me better, only I get the heartburn something terrible.'

'I'm telling you,' the baker said, 'it's the black bread. I'm a baker, shouldn't I know?'

'Hello, Joe,' Mr Kandinsky said, 'what you got there?'

'Cripple, ain't it?' said the baker.

'It'll grow,' the man said.

'Can you lend me five shillings to pay for this unicorn, Mr Kandinsky?' Joe said.

'For a unicorn,' said Mr Kandinsky, reaching for the box he kept his change in, 'five shillings is *tukke* cheap.'

Later, Mr Kandinsky made a careful examination.

'Clearly,' he said, 'this unicorn is without doubt a unicorn, Joe; unmistakably it is a genuine unicorn, Shmule. It has only one small horn budding on its head.'

'Let's see,' said Shmule. Then after he looked and felt the horn bud he said, 'Granted only one horn.'

'Second and still important,' continued Mr Kandinsky, 'Joe went to the market to buy a unicorn. That is so, Joe?'

Joe nodded.

'Consequently,' Mr Kandinsky continued excitedly, 'it follows that he wouldn't buy something that wasn't a unicorn. In which case, he bought a unicorn, which is what this is.'

'There's a lot in what you say,' replied Shmule, 'although it looks like a baby goat, a little bit crippled that's all, not like a horse which is, after all, a unicorn except for the horn.'

'And this has a horn, yes or no?' asked Mr Kandinsky.

'Definitely,' replied Shmule, 'it has an underdeveloped horn.'

'One horn only?' asked Mr Kandinsky.

'One horn,' agreed Shmule.

'So,' concluded Mr Kandinsky, 'it's not a unicorn?'

'What do I know?' said Shmule shrugging his shoulders. The shrug reminded him of his shoulder muscles, so he went on flexing and unflexing them for a while.

Then Mr Kandinsky sent Joe to the greengrocery to buy a cabbage and some carrots. 'And a couple of heads of lettuce as well,' he added. 'What he don't eat, we can put in the stew.'

While Joe was gone, Mr Kandinsky examined the unicorn again, while Shmule practised a half-Nelson on himself.

As he ran his hand over the unicorn, Mr Kandinsky sang:
One kid, one kid, which my father bought for two farthings.
Shmule looked around. 'That's what I say,' he said. 'A kid.'

'What harm will it do, Shmule,' asked Mr Kandinsky, 'if we make it a unicorn? Oy,' he added, 'he really is crippled.' Sadly beating his fist on the bench Mr Kandinsky sang:

Then came the Holy One, blessed be He,
The angel of death to destroy utterly
That struck down the butcher
That slew the ox
That drank the water
That quenched the fire
That burnt the stick
That beat the dog
That bit the cat
That ate the kid.

Shmule's low voice joined Mr Kandinsky's cracked one in the chorus. Together they finished the song.

One kid, one kid, which my father bought for two farthings.

Acknowledgements

The editor wishes to thank the authors (or their agents or trustees) and publishers who have granted permission to reproduce the following copyright material:

'His First Flight' by Liam O'Flaherty, from *The Short Stories of Liam O'Flaherty* (Jonathan Cape).

'Way-atcha the Coon-Raccoon of Kilder Creek' by Ernest Thompson Seton (Hodder & Stoughton).

'The Dog that Bit People' by James Thurber, from *Vintage Thurber* (Hamish Hamilton) and from *My Life and Hard Times* (Harper & Row, New York). © 1933, 1961 by James Thurber.

'The Miracle of Purun Bhagat' by Rudyard Kipling from *The Second Jungle Book* (Macmillan, London and Basingstoke). Reprinted by permission of the National Trust.

'The Rain Horse' by Ted Hughes, from *Wodwo* (Faber & Faber).

'The White Pony' by H. E. Bates, from *Thirty-one Selected Tales* (Jonathan Cape). Reprinted by permission of the Estate of the late H. E. Bates.

'The Unicorn' by Wolf Mankowitz, from *A Kid for Two Farthings* (André Deutsch). © 1964 by the author.